Praise for *Disrupt-It-Yourself*

"Disruption may be inevitable, but it doesn't need to be destructive. This practical, masterful approach guides large organizations to be agile by building a safe place for innovative ideas, staying close to customers and supporting the intrapreneurs who create breakthrough solutions."

—**Asheesh Saksena**, chief strategic growth officer, Best Buy

"Based on new research and practical experience, this highly readable guide shows leaders how to identify and engage the undercover innovators inside organizations to create real value for customers. This is a significant contribution to innovation ideation and execution—one you can put into practice immediately."

—**Julie Guggemos**, senior vice president, product design and development, Target

"*Disrupt-It-Yourself* engages leaders to create and unleash 'communities of innovation' as a powerful antidote to the 'business as usual' ways of working that hold organizations back from sustainable growth. An essential read for forward-looking leaders and organizations."

—**Tom Beauregard**, executive vice president and chief innovation officer, UnitedHealth Group

"Ahuja shows managers and leaders how to nurture and support innovators on the inside, giving them a safe space for bold innovation, even in highly regulated industries. *Disrupt-It-Yourself* is sure to become the new mantra for innovative organizations everywhere!"

—**Stephanie Hammes-Betti**, senior vice president, Innovation Design, US Bank

"Maintaining a startup culture in large organizations is as paramount to success as nurturing the core business. *Disrupt-It-Yourself* presents a playbook to guide large firms to create a balance of both—freedom and agility along with guidance and guardrails—so innovation can flourish with the discipline it needs to become sustainable. Don't miss out on this urgent and timely guide."

—**Yazdi Bagli**, senior vice president, Global Business Services, Walmart

"*Disrupt-It-Yourself* gives an eye-opening overview and insightful guidance on how to enable intrapreneurship, leveraging new ways for collaboration and enabling creativity that lead to meaningful and sustainable innovation."

—Eric Quint, vice president and chief design officer, 3M Company

"Meaningful solutions to society's most pressing problems come from unprecedented sources—both technological and human. *Disrupt-It-Yourself* will guide you to leverage the undercover intrapreneurs within your organization—and the right partners on the outside—to create new markets that build a better future for us all."

—Salim Ismail, ExO Works founder and chairman
and XPrize board member

"Democratized technology and connected communities are bringing forward a new crop of *Disrupt-It-Yourself* innovators. The principles outlined by Ahuja in this prescient guide remind us that simple but powerful tools, along with human ingenuity, make massive growth and scalable transformation possible for organizations of any size."

—Shashank Samant, president and CEO, GlobalLogic

"Change is happening at such a pace that many organizations will simply not survive in the long run. That is, unless they follow this essential guide for leading fast and focused innovation. A must-read."

—Greg McKeown, author of the *New York Times* bestseller
Essentialism: The Disciplined Pursuit of Less

"Ahuja gets it right. *Disrupt-It-Yourself* proves that shifting to an asset-based mindset and using fewer resources can spur creativity, autonomy, and growth. The principles outlined in this book offer a compelling way for companies founded in the twentieth century to remain relevant in the twenty-first century and beyond."

—Srinivas Prasad, CEO, Philips Innovation Campus, Bangalore

"Simone provides readers with the tools to move from being idea killers to creators of killer ideas. This is a must-read for those looking to become global intrapreneurs and those who want to foster more intrapreneur-driven innovation in their organizations."

—Hans Balmaekers, chief at Innov8rs.co

DISRUPT IT YOURSELF

DISRUPT IT YOURSELF

EIGHT WAYS TO HACK A BETTER BUSINESS—BEFORE THE COMPETITION DOES

Simone Bhan Ahuja

HarperCollins Leadership

AN IMPRINT OF HarperCollins

Published by HarperCollins Leadership, an imprint of HarperCollins Focus LLC.

Unless otherwise noted, all quotes come from the author's personal interviews and are used with permission.

ISBN 978-1-5955-4072-0 (eBook)
ISBN 978-1-5955-4049-2 (HC)
ISBN 978-1-4002-1098-5 (IE)

Library of Congress Cataloging-in-Publication Data

Library of Congress Control Number: 2018957776

Printed in the United States of America
19 20 21 22 23 LSC 10 9 8 7 6 5 4 3 2 1

For my parents—the original disrupters
For our son, Niko, a next-generation disrupter
And for my partner, Hari, who helps all of us
keep a foot on the ground, and without whom
this book would not have been possible.

Contents

Foreword

"Disrupt yourself" has become as routine in business parlance as "maximize shareholder value." They are phrases that roll off the tongue so readily and so often that one might be lulled into a false belief that their fulfillment is both easy to achieve and pervasive in companies today. In reality, they are some of the most challenging and important tasks at hand. And accomplishing them is becoming more difficult every day as the pace of technological change continues to accelerate, upending the status quo and paving the way for new, disruptive challenger products, services, and business models, which often appear with lightning speed.

The average life span of an S&P 500 company has decreased to about fifteen years, down from sixty-seven years in the 1920s, and the vast majority of Fortune 500 companies from the class of 1955 are no longer on the list. Companies and brands that were once part of our daily vernacular—Circuit City, Blockbuster, and Oldsmobile—have been replaced by companies such as Amazon,

Netflix, and Tesla. Facebook, Uber, and Airbnb have created entire new industries seemingly overnight, and for the successful companies, the gestation period from startup to multibillion market capitalization continues to shrink dramatically.

The year 2018 marked Stanley Black & Decker's 175th anniversary. We are a manufacturer that was formed in the wake of the first Industrial Revolution and has continued to innovate in order to stay relevant during the second and third. We are now in the midst of a fourth industrial revolution, which is creating exciting and daunting challenges and opportunities for us and all legacy industrial companies. This time around it is different, in the sense that the speed of change has accelerated to a point at which it is impossible—or will soon become so—for any one institution to be able to absorb the change. Achieving longevity and sustainable success in this era requires new collaborative leadership models, new skills, and new cultural attributes. The degree of difficulty has never been so steep and the stakes are sky-high. I envision a near future where the difference between business leaders who understand and actualize this and those who don't will be the defining factor in the sustainability of legacy companies.

This doesn't, however, mean turning everyone in your company into an innovation expert and dismantling what has made your organization successful. As Simone Ahuja argues in *Disrupt-It-Yourself*, it means taking the unique aspects of your company and culture and putting them to work. It means creating the internal structures for management, tapping into existing talent in addition to bringing in new ways of thinking, and creating a culture that enables speed and experimentation—one that captures the passion and purpose of your people.

Make no mistake: *intrapreneurship*, as Ahuja calls it, is no small task. When the topic is raised, many experts are right to consider the dangers of a company's "immune system" kicking in and essentially kicking out new ways of thinking and acting. It's probably the greatest danger to innovation within a large organization.

To overcome this challenge, purpose is a great starting point. When we think about the most recent class of organizations that have been formed, they often focus on an MTP or "massive transformative purpose." That purpose unites employees around a common mission and reason for being and helps align their efforts. It serves as a guidepost for decision-making when, in order to truly disrupt within an organization, some of the company's rules have to be, frankly, overruled. It helps employees connect with customers and the value-creating solutions that set the company apart from its competitors.

For Stanley Black & Decker, our purpose is "for those who make the world." As a $20-plus billion global manufacturer, we are for the makers, innovators, creators, and protectors who are out doing the hard work to make our world a better place. We support the craftsmen and the caregivers, the people on the front lines building our lives every day. We have to make the hardest-working, most innovative tools and solutions because customers depend on them for their livelihoods and for the safety and security of their workers, customers, and communities. Our people find that to be quite inspiring.

With that as the backdrop, I believe that you'll enjoy the flexible model for innovation in *Disrupt-It-Yourself* and find it immensely relevant. I met Simone about five years ago at a C-level gathering where she was speaking about innovation and intrapreneurship. She inspired me at the time, and it turned out she was prescient. Her intellect and knowledge of the subject matter are extraordinary, and her passion for it is self-evident. Much of what she believed about the subject is turning out to be absolutely correct, and she shares that knowledge in the pages that follow. We have utilized her ideas to help us define our approach to intrapreneurship and innovation and to catalyze the transformation within our company. This book offers a framework for designing an intrapreneurial program, recognizing that each organization is different and offering options to tailor the program to an enterprise's individual circumstances.

She also provides numerous examples (including some from our own company) about the hardworking people who are able to push through the boundaries that exist in traditional organizations to drive innovations over the finish line. That is no small task given the bureaucracies and hierarchies we have created over the years. Those processes and the discipline they create have been key to driving high levels of shareholder value in the past, but now a different type of leadership is required.

This new style of leadership must encourage disruption, trial and error, fast movement, constant learning, and collaborative work styles while breaking down the barriers to achievement. It has certainly asked of me, as I recently crossed sixty, a completely different approach to management and leadership—learning to let go and truly empowering our people to unleash that talent and creativity that exist within.

While we certainly don't have everything figured out at Stanley Black & Decker, all fifty-eight thousand of us are on a continuing journey of learning, applying, and relearning, and even unlearning in some cases. I encourage you to embrace the pace of change and the opportunities you have in front of you. There is only one way to continue to be relevant, and that's continuing to innovate with purpose, openness, and ever-increasing speed.

Perhaps the phrase should be "disrupt yourself and maximize shareholder value": in this day and age, you can't maximize shareholder value and ensure your long-term success unless you are working on disrupting yourself.

—Jim Loree

President & CEO

Stanley Black & Decker

Introduction

> We as large organizations have just as much a
> right to play into that future, if not more so, than
> these kids in a garage somewhere that we're
> scared of.
>
> —Kyle Nel, CEO of Uncommon Partners, former
> executive director of Lowe's Innovation Labs

I frequently find myself in animated discussions with leaders about impending disruption. They have seen repeatedly how innovations hatched by hot startups can swiftly displace incumbents and generate entirely new markets. We share ideas about how they can prepare for these disruptions and respond to the rapid shifts that are in progress. More than anything, I urge them to trigger these changes themselves. It's a part of what I call the Disrupt-It-Yourself imperative, which presupposes that the only way an organization can win in an innovation-driven economy is to invent the future itself by unleashing more of its own talent and energy.

Many of the executives I know are waking up to this imperative. They are aware that they need more intrapreneurs—people who, despite being employees, behave in many ways like entrepreneurs. But they're not sure how to create the conditions needed to attract and empower these people, much less manage the whole spectrum of innovations from incremental improvements of existing offerings to highly ambitious and groundbreaking "moonshots."

The discovery flows both ways in these conversations. I find myself leaning forward to follow up on an original insight or to commiserate with a team's grueling setbacks. And occasionally, the person across the table decides to throw me a curveball. One such moment occurred about a year ago, when a manager working in a large innovation lab broke the news to me: "That thing you're looking for? You'll never find it."

I had been unpacking my plan for this book—to look under the hood at innovation-hungry companies to discover the secret combination of structure, roles, and tools that create a powerful engine of Disrupt-It-Yourself (DIY) activity. He sighed and continued, "Seriously, the one perfect setup for supporting intrapreneurship? That icon of so-called Disrupt-It-Yourself innovation? It doesn't exist."

Fair enough. I had uncovered some impressive programs supporting streams of extremely promising initiatives, but no one had unpacked the DIY approach in a way that was clear and flawless—or truly transferrable.

And that is exactly as it should be. Not only is every DIY effort distinct but each is forever evolving. Every organization needs something slightly different. Rather than dream up an arbitrary ideal for the mythic intrapreneurial organization, I became determined to upload and translate the hidden principles that underpin the most successful approaches in practice today. As part of that, I've crafted a powerful synthesis of actionable prescriptions based on sound evidence. These are strategies that can be applied with great flexibility and can guide refinements over time. That's the winning formula.

In one sense, companies have a lot in common these days. Most are waking up to the same basic understanding that Cisco's long-time CEO, John Chambers, alluded to when he told an audience that "forty percent of businesses . . . will not exist in a meaningful way in 10 years." He went on to say: "If I'm not making you sweat, I should be. . . . Either we disrupt or we get disrupted."[1] The innovation-focused consultancy Innosight supports Chambers's conclusions with its corporate longevity forecast. It found that the big US companies that made up the S&P 500 back in 1964 tended to stay on the list for a long time—an average of thirty-three years. That tenure has done nothing but shrink since. In 2016, the average time on the list was down to twenty-four years. By 2027, forecasters predict it will be just twelve.[2] However, while over 40 percent of executives say that their company is at risk or very at risk of disruption, 78 percent of innovation portfolios are allocated to continuous (or incremental) innovation instead of disruptive risks.[3]

Meanwhile, the life cycle of products and services in competitive markets is shorter than ever. If a firm wants to grow, it is no longer enough to stamp out yesterday's widgets more efficiently. The management teams I work with are finding that yesterday's growth strategies—which often leave risky disruptive innovation to startups and then buy the ones that succeed—have lost much of their logic. Today entrepreneurs are more capable than ever of quickly scaling and capturing market share on their own, and post-merger integration is increasingly challenging, so it makes more and more sense for established organizations to enable and empower a broad spectrum of innovation on the inside—including disruptive innovation. Even Wall Street and boards of directors are increasingly pressuring CEOs to drive internal disruption by making big, risky bets that could upend the company and industry, while simultaneously maintaining core business. But many organizations and leaders lack confidence in their abilities to do so. When PricewaterhouseCoopers (PwC) surveyed managers in a wide range of companies in 2013, it found a small minority of "most innovative" firms expected, on average, to see growth of 62 percent over five years and a much larger "least innovative" group that expected just 21 percent—in other words, an annualized growth rate of 3.9 percent.[4] McKinsey & Company found a similar level of pessimism in its Global Innovation Survey. Although 84 percent of executives who responded agreed that innovation was important to their growth strategy, a mere 6 percent said they were satisfied with their organizations' innovation performance.[5] Most recognized that, unfortunately, they are sitting in companies that are highly optimized for producing yesterday's offerings as opposed to discovering tomorrow's.

There is a common phrase that many of these leaders use. One senior manager I interviewed put it this way: "Our CEO said, 'You know, I'm worried. I don't want us to have a Kodak moment.'" The CEO's reference, of course, was to Kodak's precipitous decline into irrelevance after a technology revolution destroyed its business model—the kind of collapse no CEO wants to preside over. She continued, "I think all big companies right now are in that same boat. Everybody I talk to has had a similar experience where somebody at the senior level has said, 'We need to make sure that we're not caught off guard, taken by surprise by some new company that starts up.' And that's why this group I am in was created."

She's right, and hers is hardly the only internal innovation group hatched in response to this pressure. Programs are in place in hundreds of firms, in different stages of development. But, until recently, many had assumed that a sufficient amount of innovation would spring up naturally, without any particular effort to support it in a systematic way. Now they find they are losing talent, lagging in competitive markets, and bleeding brand equity. Faced with the very real threat of seeing their core business lines disrupted, they recognize they must adopt and maintain a Disrupt-It-Yourself—or DIY—approach. They have come to realize that more of their innovation must be "organic"—seeded, grown, and successfully harvested by the firm that will benefit from it.

What kind of enterprise is capable of bringing breakthrough innovation to market with a DIY approach? Any organization can, provided it starts with a serious resolve to

1. build a strong internal structure for innovation and growth management, investing in a well-balanced innovation portfolio that will provide a sustainable edge;
2. harness the creativity and knowledge of people at all ranks and across all parts of the organization, building supportive systems and processes to leverage human strengths;
3. shift the prevailing culture to one that enables and celebrates experimentation with fast and frugal solutions and agile responses to dynamic conditions; and
4. develop leadership capable of engaging and retaining the people most committed to solving the problems of the future, and securing the enterprise's place in it.

While many companies are facing similar challenges, they also have a host of differences. They are vastly distinct in their capabilities and cultures. They have varying infrastructures and incentive schemes. They are led by different personalities, draw talent from different pools, and collaborate with different partners. All are complex entities made up of many moving parts. Whatever intrapreneurial practices work for them must work in the contexts of their unique situations. There is no single one-size-fits-all solution, and there can't be.

In this book, I present a flexible model based on my research and experience with companies learning to disrupt themselves while they carry on their everyday operations. To make these ideas immediately actionable, I identify eight key principles, analyze why they are so important, and show how organizations can put them to work at once.

Principle 1: Keep It Frugal

Many successful DIY initiatives have been pet projects pursued on shoestring budgets, if any budget at all. This limitation turns out to be beneficial to them in many ways. In situations where more resources could be thrown at early-stage ideas, teams should resist calls for funding that will bring more scrutiny, more impatience, and less ingenuity in tapping internal assets and networks. Keeping it frugal is consistent with seeking massive returns, especially initially, and can help organizations to disrupt internally.

Principle 2: Make It Permissionless

The intrapreneur's classic motto is "Ask for forgiveness, not for permission." Choosing not to go by the book on company policies and processes and instead finding back channels is often the only way to pursue a new opportunity. But not every employee capable of intrapreneurship is in a position to take on that level of personal risk. I see the companies most focused on innovative disruption bending their own rules to allow people to take their ideas further without seeking permission or having it denied. As Jim Loree mentions in the foreword of this book, "In order to truly disrupt within an organization, some of the company's rules have to be, frankly, overruled."

Principle 3: Let Customers Lead

One of the greatest advantages that intrapreneurs have over entrepreneurs is access to a large base of customers who represent the market for a new product, service, or business model and who could provide feedback critical to its development. Turning this theoretical advantage into a real one is an essential mission for companies seeking more internal innovation, and it is a big part of the rationale for establishing formal incubation and accelerator programs to become a Disrupt-It-Yourself organization.

Principle 4: Make It Fluid

The entrepreneurial community is able to respond more nimbly than large enterprises to new market opportunities in part because they can quickly pull together the team, funding, and other resources that make sense in a given situation. Large organizations should not assume it is impossible for them to operate in this fluid manner. DIY organizations can create platforms and policies to respond in agile ways to ad hoc needs.

Principle 5: Maximize Return on Intelligence

Part of creating a discipline for disruption is determining how to measure success: only with reliable metrics can you know if you are doing better at any activity this year than last. But the metrics designed for a Disrupt-It-Yourself approach cannot be the same ones used to guide the management of mature businesses. They must be applied with the same rigor as performance measurement in other areas of the business but be focused, in early stages, on maximizing learning from experimentation.

Principle 6: Create the Commons

If the idea is to create more avenues for innovation in an organization, it cannot be treated as an activity for the elite. Democratizing progress is a growing trend in society in general, and a key tenet of most enterprises' formal Disrupt-It-Yourself programs.

Principle 7: Engage Passion and Purpose

Passion is one of those words that hard-nosed managers tend to shy away from. It sounds too subjective, too laden with emotion, and too soft to be taken seriously as a target for managerial interventions. Yet the passion that comes with a sense of purpose is undeniably at the heart of the greatest Disrupt-It-Yourself success stories. Any effort to systematically encourage a spectrum of internal innovation cannot overlook it; the most sophisticated and effective programs I know are figuring out how to help people discover and channel their passion as well as inspire others with it.

Principle 8: Add Discipline to Disruption

If well managed and disciplined, multiple streams of innovation can reinforce one another to produce sustainable growth. As part of that, leaders and organizations must embrace hybridity in their innovation capabilities by simultaneously capitalizing on valuable opportunities for the near to midterm and developing fundamentally transformational ideas and technologies for the future. This is not an either/or situation; no one should see the incremental innovation of the core, which yields steady performance gains, as an alternative to the bold moves and big bets required for disruptive transformation. Both are needed.

Each of these principles is important on its own and has produced its share of valuable innovations. But it's the whole set that collectively constitutes the playbook I am sharing with you. After two context-setting chapters—the first describing who intrapreneurs are and what moves them, and the second exploring the organizational barriers that make it so hard for intrapreneurs to innovate and for companies to develop rich DIY portfolios—the bulk of this book offers chapters devoted to each of the eight principles, with stories of how each has been customized and operationalized to fit organizations of all sizes and types.

Together, the principles constitute a powerful and practical framework for designing a Disrupt-It-Yourself organization. Having this DIY playbook in hand is your first leap to bringing more predictability—and greater success—to internal innovation, leveraging your people's ingenuity, and creating an intrapreneurial culture fueled by passion and purpose. It makes a strong case for a structured process, yet it relies on experimentation within that process and iterates from there to yield solutions that are more built-to-purpose and valuable. This is a fluid approach. It can be tailored to your enterprise's circumstances and meet the needs of your shareholders and stakeholders in a way that your core business simply cannot.

Creating a Disrupt-It-Yourself system that suits your needs begins with a deep understanding of people—both the intrapreneurs trying to accomplish great things and the customers, current and potential, with needs to be met. With that in mind, this book is packed with protagonists—the constructive disrupters behind countless new products, services, features, and ways of working within their organizations.

You have protagonists like these in your own world too. Seek them out, talk to them about the principles outlined here, and collaborate with them on the best methods of application. You share a deep interest in the future success of your enterprise. None of you want to see its products, services, or business model rendered obsolete by outside disrupters. Collectively you have the knowledge to imagine new solutions and the means to make those ideas real. By working together, you can apply these principles and disrupt-it-yourself.

disrupt-it-yourself v. to launch a spectrum of high-impact innovation from within an established organization; to use a fast and frugal approach common to an entrepreneurial startup to invent a valuable new solution that finds a mass market; to enlist others in the process and refuse to be disrupted externally.

DIYer n. a Disrupt-It-Yourself innovator; an employee who acts and behaves more like an entrepreneur in the context of an established organization; a contemporary version of the traditional intrapreneur.

ONE

Navy SEALs, Not Pirates:
Meet the DIY Disrupters

"This stuff makes my skin look like chalk." That was thirteen-year-old Balanda Atis's immediate reaction when she looked at herself in the mirror.

Trying on makeup is a rite of passage for many teenage girls, and that made it all the more disappointing for Atis when she applied liquid foundation for the first time and found the results unimpressive. Cosmetics companies, it turned out, didn't make shades that suited her skin tone. Atis and her Haitian American friends in East Orange, New Jersey, found that liquid and powder foundations had an unattractive, ashy-white effect on their darker skin. It was a problem regardless of brand, formula, or product—until Atis set her sights on solving it.

When Atis joined L'Oréal USA as a chemist in 1999, she was formulating mascara, but the foundation issue weighed on her mind. In 2006, when the company launched a new line of foundations intended to address a wider variety of skin tones, Atis saw that they still didn't measure up. It lit a fire under her. She informed the head of L'Oréal's makeup division, who challenged her to come up with a solution. Atis began to work on the problem as a side project. In short order she enlisted two other scientists at L'Oréal to join her cause.

Although Atis and her colleagues were not freed from doing their day jobs, L'Oréal gave the trio access to a lab. Fueled by passion and purpose, they produced and tested foundation samples on their own time. Lacking opportunities for data collection, they tagged along on trips to existing conferences and fairs across the country, collecting skin tone measurements from thousands of women of color. The big breakthrough came when Atis discovered they could work with an existing color compound. Ultramarine blue was seldom used in cosmetics and difficult to work with, but it allowed them to create richer, deeper shades without the muddy finish that was so common in existing darker foundations. Atis and her tiny team succeeded in satisfying a massive customer need that had existed for generations.

Atis is what the business world has come to recognize as an intrapreneur. Gifford Pinchot III coined the term back in the late 1970s when he wrote about the growing number of corporate employees behaving like entrepreneurs. He even envisioned a new kind of commercial enterprise—"something akin to free market entrepreneurship within the corporate organization"— and a new way of doing business that "would be a social invention of considerable importance, both for the individuals in it, and for the productivity and responsivity of the corporation."[1]

One of Pinchot's favorite examples, and mine, is Art Fry, the 3M employee who famously invented Post-it Notes. When Fry "was told by the marketing division his idea wasn't wanted by customers, he did his own market research," Pinchot wrote. "When manufacturing told him his Post-It Notes were impossible to make, even though he worked in the lab, he worked out the production technology himself and, in blatant disregard of the rules, borrowed and re-engineered a 3M production line at night to prove his process would work. No problem, no matter how far from his supposed area of expertise as a lab person, fell outside his responsibility." Pinchot's summation that "the intrapreneur is the general manager of a new idea that doesn't yet exist" also sounds like an apt description of Balanda Atis.[2]

But Atis and others like her today are also different from the intrapreneurs of decades ago. They're more diverse in their skill sets and backgrounds, more digitally native, more networked and connected, and more ambitious to do bigger things—and they are increasingly supported by the emerging function of innovation within large organizations. Art Fry and the intrapreneurs Pinchot identified were products of long careers in their employers' organizations, and they had significant credibility and even some resources at their command. But the whole point of coining the term *intrapreneur* was to stress that there are people outside the corner office who could bring about valuable change.

Fast-forward a few decades and the democratizing trend has continued to the point where intrapreneurs can be found deeper in the ranks of organizations, pursuing high-impact ideas and making serious headway, often with collaborators they've enlisted on their own, and at times even within innovation systems created by their organizations. Compare that to the past, when a lone engineer or solo creative might have tinkered with a solution after hours, trying to keep it under wraps until it was perfected. In the old model, this person's efforts were rarely encouraged by management, much less planned or accounted for as part of the organization's official research and development agenda.

Now the reality in many firms is quite different. Today employees with varied skill sets and backgrounds work in fluid, multifunctional teams, attracting positive attention and pursuing breakthroughs that are aligned with their organizations' innovation priorities. And the most innovative firms deeply understand the need to create space and add light structure to accelerate their efforts.

It is tempting to want to give people like Balanda Atis a new name. I like to call them DIYers. We could also say they are "corporate hackers," to underline their talent of tapping into and around the bureaucratic machinery surrounding them to advance their projects. Or we could call them "constructive disrupters," since today's intrapreneurs often don't stop at trying to tweak the performance of the existing business. Sometimes they seriously challenge it, from product offering to business model, yet they do it actively from the inside and, by doing this, help keep the enterprise viable.

Whatever we call them, companies need more intrapreneurs, and their DIY initiatives, to succeed. Innovation is a clear driver of growth in today's complex and fast-moving markets. With that in mind, it makes sense to understand just who these people are, how they work, and what makes them tick.

The New Intrapreneurs Are DIYers

If Art Fry was the prototypical intrapreneur of the 1970s, and Balanda Atis represents the twenty-first-century DIY approach to intrapreneurship, what has fundamentally changed?

Intrapreneurship was . . .	Disrupt-It-Yourself is . . .
Higher-ranking, tenured executives, but constrained by working within departmental silos	People deeper in the ranks, connected to resources and knowledge through networks inside and outside the company
Focused on enhancing existing products or launching related services	Targeting new markets and novel solutions—even if they require new business models that threaten current revenue streams
A lone genius working solo	Enthusiastic collaborators who recruit like-minded colleagues with diverse skills, and who know how to navigate their organization
A creative who sees innovation as an art	Any employee who sees innovation as a systematic way to solve a problem or forge the future
An engineer or scientist by training	Employees with multidisciplinary backgrounds, deeply empathetic to customer needs
An established employee who seemed reliably grounded in the company's past	Members of diverse communities, which the enterprise recognizes as key to its future
An employee in a big corporation	An employee in an organization large or small, for-profit, nonprofit, or in the public sector

An individual whose life circumstances allowed them to burn the midnight oil, unpaid for the extra hours	A person whose passion for an idea drives them to start a side project, and ultimately the wise enterprise may provide material support
Driven by intrinsic rewards, extrinsic rewards not an option	Driven by intrinsic rewards, and propelled further when smart organizations offer options for extrinsic rewards

The Intrapreneurial Archetype

If you could hire a hundred Balandas tomorrow, you would do it, right? What better move could you make to ensure your company's relevance in the future? We've already heard the stats and predictions about how vulnerable today's largest and most longstanding companies are. And as fund managers like to put it, their past performance is no guarantee of future results. Highfliers routinely end up crashing down to earth. So if you don't want your business to join the countless others already consigned to the dustbin of history, at some point you'll have to disrupt it yourself—and your best chance of doing that is to grow, develop, and support your ranks of intrapreneurs.

Unfortunately, you probably couldn't hire those hundred Balandas if you tried—not because these talented disrupters wouldn't work for your company but because it's hard to find them in the labor market. There are no job titles or specific functional areas reserved for people who spot opportunities and jump on them. It's tough for the HR department, or software tools scanning applications, to zero in on the résumé line that shows whether someone thinks like an entrepreneur. And it can be challenging to spot the intrapreneurs who are already sitting inside your organization. They're definitely there, some of them making progress on side hustles no one even knows about, and many more of them with valuable ideas they would like to pursue.

Is it possible that there is nothing remarkable about intrapreneurs as individuals—that most of us, with enough encouragement and confidence, could succeed in challenging the status quo? That's a key message, for example, of Adam Grant's recent bestseller, *Originals*, and I couldn't agree more with his goal to create more creatives. But as most knowledge workers look across their workplaces, they don't see a landscape densely populated by mavericks. Intrapreneurs are still relatively rare, distinguished by both who they are and what they do.[3] So, if we did list the job qualifications for the intrapreneurs, the innovators you would want on the inside of your organization, it would look like this:

- **Action obsessed.** Forward-thinking and optimistic, intrapreneurs are energized by what hasn't been done before. Think of Balanda Atis, undeterred by the fact that a global industry with all its resources had not solved the problem she saw. She forged ahead anyway, finding partners, doing the science, cultivating a community of internal supporters, and generally taking every step in her power to pursue her idea with passion.
- **Progress focused.** Intrapreneurs are impatient with systems that put the brakes on progress. Dakota Crow, an experienced innovation leader who is currently VP of Innovation and director of the Innovator-in-Residence program at US bank, told me about the frustration people feel when their momentum is blocked by well-intentioned

managers adhering to process: "If you're pushing on a product or idea and you've got enough validation to move forward, stopping is like someone saying, 'Wait—pull the car over. We've got to change the tires.' You're like, 'I've got plenty of tread!'" The next words out of his mouth could have been uttered by any one of the intrapreneurs I've met: "I'm just not a fan of process for the sake of process."

- **Problem oriented.** Despite their bias for action, intrapreneurs don't accept the first solution they arrive at just to be done with the job. They go through iterations working the problem, attacking it from different angles, and challenging the assumptions that might constrain their thinking. A favorite phrase of Intuit leaders comes to mind: the most creative people "fall in love with the problem, not the solution."[4] Intrapreneurs understand that there are typically multiple answers to every problem and many paths to any solution. They are learners, scanning all sources for information that can advance their progress.

- **Natural hackers.** In software, hackers love the intellectual challenge of confronting a system designed to do certain things and cleverly exploiting it to achieve something different. Likewise, intrapreneurs overcome the limitations of an organization by bending its strengths to their will. A senior marketing manager at an American candy manufacturer is a fountain of new product ideas in need of customer validation. Yet customers are often treated like a protected species by those who "own" these relationships—sometimes they are completely off-limits. So this intrapreneurial manager hacked a simple solution. "An organization with several thousand employees has access to at least several thousand *consumers*," he surmised.

(Especially an organization that creates and distributes candy.) On any given day, he can walk around and get a "semi-outsider" perspective on new ideas by inviting feedback from employees. He hacked a good solution to what otherwise is a stubborn problem.

- **Talent attractors.** Calling intrapreneurs "hackers" might summon up the image of a lone genius chipping away at a pet project in isolation—on the contrary, they are by necessity and temperament radically inclusive. They engage in open-source partnering and codesign solutions with end users and other stakeholders. When I asked Bob Schwartz, GE Healthcare's global design chief, about this intrapreneurial trait, he told me: "There are so many stakeholders needed to get anything out the door in any manufacturing environment—and they have to be co-owners with you." If that means you spend a lot of time "waving your hands over your head" evangelizing your idea, while making it as much as you can about them, he said, so be it. This is a theme that cuts across most of the DIY efforts I studied: Intrapreneurs don't try to go it alone. They reach across the aisle to complementary areas where they need help and enlist others by making it clear what's in it for them.

- **Married to mission.** Intrapreneurs are often cast as an organization's heretics, but the thing to understand is that they are frequently the most devout believers in its mission. Their problem is with how the mission is being translated into strategy and tactics. Ian Stephenson, who made a career out of being a maverick at Cargill, stressed this point. He said, "Entrepreneurialism inside a large organization is about identifying gaps and misalignments, and better aligning the organization so it performs better."

In this formulation, the deviator from the strategy paradoxically keeps the company on track. Stephenson went on to say, "[Intrapreneurship] is being married to a purpose but not necessarily married to a way to do it. You know the what and the why—it's just the how that you want to be able to play across."

- **Frugal by nature.** Like hackers, intrapreneurs proceed on the cheap, reusing existing resources, recycling materials, and employing messy, make-do methods over expensive, sanctioned systems. They are resourceful and don't ask for much—even when more would be granted.

I was struck by Babak Forutanpour's response when higher-ups at Qualcomm expressed an eagerness to support the grassroots innovation movement he had nurtured from one team of eight to ultimately thousands of employees on dozens of teams working over lunchtimes and weekends. He recalls, "We all agreed: let's just ask for a little pizza and beer money." The figure he went back with was $7,000—giving the fourteen teams $500 each to cover takeout. The point is simple: the classic engineering bias toward getting maximum output from minimum input is in these internal disrupters' bones.

From action-oriented to mission-driven and frugal, that's seven key attributes—and there's more, since intrapreneurs are also resourceful, thick-skinned, and resilient. Of course, it's a lot to expect from any single individual—and the truth is that every innovator has his or her own particular strengths and preferred modes of working. Back in 1980, Karl Vesper made this point about entrepreneurs too—that it was more useful to understand that they come in many flavors than to try to pin down their collective "type." He came up with at least eight varieties, many of which overlap with my findings.[5] That's part of why Marc Nager, managing director at Telluride Venture Accelerator and former CEO of Startup Weekend, says that good teams usually come in threes. "You need the person with the structure who can operate things," he says, "but also need the visionary, and then the executor. In other words: the hipster, the hacker, and the hustler."

The Bottom Line

So what's a classic intrapreneur? An employee who isn't necessarily given the setup and top-down mandate to create something new and valuable but starts doing it anyway. Intrapreneurs are the people who are just doing their jobs when they discover needs that are not being met by their organization. They are the internal disrupters who see the possibility of addressing those problems from where they sit, and they begin finding their ways to solutions. They make progress by enlisting others, achieving small victories, and pushing ahead, for the most part under the radar. That classic entrepreneurial story of someone starting a company in their garage with fifty dollars? Translate that to someone inside a company, and that's also the classic story of intrapreneurship.

These people have always existed in large organizations. Historically, they have been somewhat taken for granted, and occasionally appreciated—in other words, they have been tolerated. Today, large organizations understand the need for constant innovation, and for the first time intrapreneurs are starting to be developed, recruited, systematically supported, and celebrated.

So there is great reason to feel hopeful for the future, in spite of all the doomsday scenarios painted about large companies.

Intrapreneurs are more able to make headway and add value than ever before—especially in organizations that recognize their value—and, along with forward-looking leaders, help pave a path to a Disrupt-It-Yourself organization.

It's incumbent upon leaders to identify the disrupters the company should be supporting better, while also building the systems and driving the culture change that will produce more of them.

TWO

Why Does It Have to Be So Hard?

Intrapreneurs, the innovative employees who help large organizations drive innovation and at times even disrupt themselves, aren't the same as entrepreneurs on the outside. They're not your typical corporate employees either: some do, in fact, leave big organizations to commercialize ideas on their own. Those who go that route follow a well-worn path—one taken by Steve Wozniak, for example, when he left Hewlett Packard to build the first Apple computer (he moonlighted on the task for a while before his departure); by Robert Noyce when he felt he wasn't getting enough traction at Shockley Semiconductor and walked away to start Fairchild Semiconductor (and later Intel); and for that matter, by Shockley Semiconductor's own founder, William Shockley, who made his mark at Bell Labs before he chose to go his own way.

These are well-known cases, and they have many elements in common with others I've seen. Capable people work to build startling advancements in staid firms. They bring together communities that have common hopes and challenges and are willing to float ideas and resources. They are enabled by technology and motivated by passion and purpose. That passion can also spark their departure if they don't receive the support they need.

This risk of intrapreneurial flight is only rising. As new startups emerge every day, and barriers to entry continue to fall, entrepreneurship begins to seem less exceptional and more like a proper path for anyone with an idea and the confidence to pursue it. At times, these disrupters feel they must leave in order to pursue their passion. Short of deciding to launch their own businesses, intrapreneurs exit for other familiar reasons. Some move on when another company steps up to offer a tempting platform and position, one with more assets and a greater appreciation for people and their bright ideas. Others leave out of simple frustration.

In no way do I want to single out any one company when key executives leave to pursue an innovation on their own. If only I could single out just one—if only the problem were limited to just a few companies. In fact, all the symptoms—the layers of decision-making, budget constraints, and problematic incentives—are typical of big companies. It's like this: if this were a zombie movie, we'd be at the point in the second hour when most of the world has been infected and the few survivors that have managed to protect their vitality, creativity, and agility are the hardy exceptions.

Before we cut to the chase and see how those few companies enable sustainable intrapreneurship, we need to understand what cuts it to the quick in so many others. The diagnosis comes down to two kinds of problems, some created by the structure of large organizations, and others due to the mind-sets that take hold in them. As we look at these structural and mind-set barriers in their various forms, we'll learn that no one is actively trying to kill innovation. People are behaving rationally, and almost all of them with good intentions. The problem is that they are deciding and acting within a context, and the system around them is arrayed in complex ways against the forces of innovation.

The First, Worst Barrier: Mind-Set

Having said that nobody is actively trying to kill innovation, I should quickly add that it doesn't always feel that way. People with great ideas for making their employers better often get the sense that someone is out to get them—and that someone is usually their immediate boss. Sure, in a layer far above them, top management might be broadcasting positive messages that invite them to (or even insist that they) "behave more entrepreneurially" and "invent the future" and "save us all from crushing, humiliating irrelevancy." But when they take top management at its word, they learn just how far away that top layer is, *and* how close the manager is whose main goal is to keep them focused on the work they were expressly hired to perform.

This is what Babak Forutanpour was up against as a software engineer at Qualcomm circa 2004. Once he was onboarded and unpacked his laptop, he realized there was no suitable place to bring a new idea to have it vetted and considered for development. "No one was listening, and my boss didn't even want to brainstorm," he recalled.

Eventually he was so desperate for a sounding board that he pulled together a "little biweekly luncheon" with like-minded people outside his usual circle. "If nothing else," he figured, they could all "eat a ham sandwich with someone interesting." But that initial group quickly decided to go beyond the sandwich and try to accomplish something more substantial together. In short order they came up with a cool new technical solution for reducing ambient noise. After a thorough vetting of prototypes by subject-matter experts, a patent that eventually produced real value for Qualcomm was applied for and awarded. That filing was followed by more, and Forutanpour found himself the accidental founder of a movement within the company.

The group acquired a name—FLUX, for "forward-looking user experience"—and it started spawning many new lunch-group teams in its wake. That's when Forutanpour experienced the type of active resistance that stops innovation in its tracks. The same manager who was uninterested in his ideas now wanted him to stop using his free time to develop them. "Shut it down," his boss said.

At this point, Forutanpour became even more effusive—demonstrating just how much intrapreneurs like him care about their work and what matters. Suffice it to say, he got himself out of that reporting relationship and went to work in another part of the organization. And FLUX kept growing, from eight people to more than three thousand, meeting on four continents and capturing seventy patents in about seventy months.[1]

Not every disrupter on the inside could snatch victory so decidedly away from defeat as Forutanpour did. As we see here, top management in many companies emphasizes ideation and initiative, yet people can't get traction with their own supervisors. The entrepreneurial mind-set is shallow and intermittent at best.

In a 2013 survey of corporate professionals by Accenture, only 20 percent said their managers encourage entrepreneurial ideas.[2] That mind-set barrier has destructive effects on two levels. First, it robs the company of any immediate innovations those intrapreneurs were imagining. Second, it drives away those who represent the organization's best chance of innovating more in the future. Plenty of other studies show that when people leave jobs, they are not choosing to leave companies so much as they are choosing to leave bosses.[3] I suspect this is especially true for intrapreneurs. So it's tempting to say to employers, "Get rid of those toxic managers so this mind-set issue is alleviated."

However, the modern corporation has made managers who they are. Think for a moment about how middle managers are incented, and it becomes clear that very little about intrapreneurship serves them well. They have solid reasons for not helping people pursue these dreams: any amount of time spent on activity that isn't mandated by senior leadership is time taken away from the entire team's tightly defined performance objectives. Beyond concerns about ROI, a host of other barriers emerge, including fear that support of such initiatives will be penalized rather than rewarded, not to mention a host of cultural issues, such as innovation initiatives not being taken seriously.

Betting on long shots is fine at the level of the enterprise—in fact, from a whole-portfolio view you must lay a lot of bets and accept that most won't pay off. But at the work-group level, those odds look terrible, and managers have every reason to adopt a play-it-safe mind-set. This is where mind-set and structural barriers come together.

The Second Serious Barrier: Structure

The boss's perspective is a big problem for intrapreneurs, but the barriers in the typical large company go beyond mind-set and come right down to its structural underpinning. According to Vijay Anand, senior vice president at Intuit, it's not a lack of desire that blocks companies from supporting entrepreneurship; it's just the way they are wired. According to Anand, "Large organizations are necessarily focused on running the business and managing for continuity. That's not always a bad thing, but it seldom leaves much space for new ways of working."

Organizations finely tuned to accomplish certain things in certain ways lose their ability to imagine other possibilities. The old expression goes, "The fish cannot see the water it swims in." That's a great metaphor for people working in contexts where assumptions about what a market wants and how an organization should respond have firmly taken hold. These become givens in their thinking, not even considered as conditions that could be different.

I wholeheartedly agree with Larry Keeley of Doblin, who told me this: "Every time somebody tells me, 'We've got cultural obstacles to innovation,' what I usually say is, 'Well, maybe—but let me first show you all the things that are standing in the way in terms of incentives, metrics, and rewards. And once we fix all that, then you can tell me if we've fixed your culture, or if we've fixed the mechanics of how you innovate.'"

Let's look at a few of these structural barriers to see what they amount to collectively.

Lack of Slack

First, we have to admit that in the less global, less hyper-competitive markets of the past, firms had more slack in their operations. Exploratory projects and experiments that might never pan out could more easily be indulged. But these days, slack rarely exists because efficiency-minded management systems have gotten so good at identifying and eliminating it.

Slack is more than a brand of collaboration software. Among organizational theorists, it's a term of art and a matter of deep interest. For example, Nitin Nohria, the dean of Harvard Business School, writing with Ranjay Gulati, defined it as "the pool of resources in an organization that is in excess of the minimum necessary to produce a given level of organizational output," and he is absolutely convinced of its importance to innovation.[4] Basically, Nohria and Gulati's finding is this: when an organization is run as a very tight ship, it gets today's work done with great efficiency, but it doesn't manage to discover what it could do differently tomorrow. Accenture's 2013 survey (cited previously) asked employees to single out the biggest barrier to entrepreneurialism in their companies. The top answer was that their jobs kept them too busy to pursue new ideas.[5] Wayne Morris, an innovation director at enterprise software maker SAP, told me that "in a software engineering-type organization, you always have developers who have pet projects they work on after hours and on weekends." But when they bring these concepts to their managers, he said, they are likely to hear: "Thanks for the idea— but your job is to focus on your deliverables of X, Y, and Z."

Lack of slack is why so many of today's intrapreneurs do their thing on their own time. And belief in slack is why a few firms, starting with 3M, have tried offering employees "20 percent time" or some version of it, granting people a chunk of their workweek to lay aside formal assignments and pursue projects they think have potential. Essentially, these internal disrupters are trying to engineer in the slack that organizations have worked so hard to engineer out.

The Metrics Question

Companies have gained a lot of sophistication and precision over the years in how they measure success. Once upon a time, this was done with the pedantic process of waiting till the end of the year, letting the accountants sum everything up, and finally seeing that revenues exceeded costs—hooray! (Or didn't—start cost cutting immediately!) Everyone realized the shortcoming in this situation, that the measures didn't happen at a level or with a timeliness to suggest smart course corrections. Measurement science came a long way during the total quality management movement, when work processes came under the microscope and all the various steps of value creation in a business had "metrics" applied to them. That had the desired effect, and the easiest way to sum up the result is with the now-famous phrase: "What gets measured gets managed."

A lot about the creative process, however, is fuzzy and doesn't lend itself to tight specification. If an executed idea innovation doesn't end up setting the world on fire, it's usually impossible to point to the assembly-line step where the defect was introduced and some diligent worker should have yanked the pull cord. So metrics were devised, and performance measurement systems and worker incentives got attached to them. But they were applied to the parts of an organization's work that were engineered for predictability and efficiency—not to the messiness of innovation. In Stanford emeritus professor James March's words, the corporation became a machine more engineered for exploitation than exploration.[6]

At a Fortune 50 retailer, one executive told me how "the metrics question" comes up in innovation initiatives and undermines the more visionary and radical projects. It's hard enough to come up with a yardstick when an effort doesn't map neatly to an established profit-and-loss (P&L) center—which disruptive innovations rarely do. Things get even dicier when the goals are set up within a broader corporate framework that is all about maximizing shareholder value.

In principle, there should be no reason that a desire to meet a fiduciary responsibility to shareholders would cut off investments in innovation. What could serve them better? But it all depends on timelines and incentives. Senior leaders are classically rewarded by stock performance, which in turn leads to a focus on quarterly results. In this scenario it's better to focus on short-term cost cutting and incremental changes than longer-term moonshots. The short-term-ism that has taken hold in the capital markets has drained investors' patience with ideas that require funds to develop and don't pay off fast. Company boards and Wall Street finally seem to be getting it, but for a long time the Street has rewarded only cost cutting or quick incremental improvements with immediate revenue gain, and has been cruel to firms visibly attempting to disrupt themselves. Case in point: when Target handed out pink slips in 2017, it was because, in CEO Brian Cornell's words, "our focus on innovation has to be something we can realize over the next three or four years inside the core business."[7] The most high-profile departures were from the special group the firm created to explore the future of retail and launch highly innovative experiments.

This is part of why we have seen a wave of companies going private. When I asked Salim Ismail—serial tech entrepreneur, ExO Works founder and chairman, and XPRIZE board member—his advice for a company wishing to be more disruptive, he said, "Number one: get off the public market and take it private. . . . You can't do something radically different if you're having to meet your quarterly Wall Street numbers. It's just not possible." Short of that, Bob Schwartz of GE Healthcare spells out what intrapreneurs have to learn if they want to take a DIY approach in a Fortune 500 environment. "They're all big, corporate meat grinders," he says, "and they have to deliver to Wall Street—constantly." When you're dealing with someone who has P&L responsibility, your goal shouldn't be to get them to forget the bottom line. It won't happen. The key is to understand why investing feels so risky to them. In his innovation-focused Global Design group, Schwartz says that pressure is something "we all know and we understand. And we have respect for it."

Unfortunately, when top management has its eyes focused on the next quarter's results, innovation gets lip service that doesn't get translated into performance objectives and incentives.

The Alignment Conundrum

What else could drive a manager to look away from a novel idea? Often, it's a lack of clear innovation strategy. In a professionally managed company, performance objectives align with a strategic plan that has been devised up high and cascaded down through the organization. Execution is the key to success, and management is already challenged to communicate strategy through the ranks effectively—and new approaches without clear strategy add complexity rather than value.

The more closely a company stays focused on its core business, the less supportive it is of experimental forays. Strategies often come with stretch goals, which will require everyone rowing hard together; so, this resistance, often called the "corporate immune system," becomes much more active when an intrapreneur's idea sounds like it falls outside "business as usual" practices and into DIY, especially if it cannibalizes an existing line of business. If a proposed change presents that kind of risk, managers need proof that it will pay off—with a bigger return than what is already in place. These objections can be at the heart of what I heard one Intuit intrapreneur call "the alignment conundrum"—that built-in problem that an employee's new idea "is not aligned with our strategy."

Larry Keeley tells me this is one of the most common and, to him, ridiculous excuses that managers in big companies invoke to reject a fledgling innovation. "It's the same cliché rejection pattern that you hear all the time," he says. "Managers say, 'This is great, but it just doesn't move the needle'—by which they mean it won't produce $100 million in incremental revenues this year." Meanwhile, he points out, all those start-up businesses that "aren't living inside of a corporation are very happy with, let's say, a first-year success of $20 million." The fact that big companies "have a higher jump bar before they even notice" a promising idea means they miss out on most opportunities until the chance to get in on the ground floor is lost. They don't see the strategic case for encouraging the initiative, so they kill it off.

Of course it's important to have strategic objectives that everyone understands as well as a path laid out for achieving them. But if tactics are too precise and exclude innovation entirely, then execution leaves no room for improvisation, and this rigidity becomes the enemy of innovation.

The Bureaucracy Barrier

One of the biggest and most consistent structural barriers to a Disrupt-It-Yourself approach turns out to be bureaucracy and standard operating procedures. By the time a company has reached any scale, it has figured out how to organize itself to achieve consistent, high-quality output. Certain roles have to be filled and steps followed. But at some point, the focus on "how we do things around here" becomes a fixation, with managers devoting more attention to process than to product.

Marc Nager recalls some would-be entrepreneurs who came to the Startup Weekend events he used to lead. Many times, they came armed with laptops fully loaded with project management tools and techniques. But they "got hung up on all these sophisticated solutions and they overcomplicated a lot," Nager says. "We came in and said, 'Use sticky notes.'"

Managers are pinned to process for various reasons. Process is an essential thing to prop up bureaucracy. Bureaucracy is a very effective way to limit access to the valuable assets of the enterprise—and one of the easiest ways to shut down something that was "not invented here."

There is a great irony in this. As we've seen, intrapreneurs often choose to stay in corporate settings because they see the opportunity to deploy the strong assets of established businesses—the customer access, the supply chain relationships, the resident expertise, and more. And companies with underutilized assets are in dire need of new, more valuable ways to deploy them. Yet the two sides can't connect, because the assets are so effectively cordoned off by processes and bureaucracy. As Deloitte puts it, "the hierarchical and inflexible structures within organizations often ignore or actively suppress ideas that are created bottom-up."[8]

Overriding the Organizational Immune System

Hallmark Cards art director Gordon MacKenzie famously described his employer as "the giant hairball" that any employee who wanted to do creative work had to learn to orbit.[9]

It's an apt term for describing the system an intrapreneur is up against in the typical corporation. It's easy to make the diagnosis but much tougher to unravel, disarm, or override the symptoms. And this immune system can be overcome—with the right approach.

This book takes the optimistic but realistic position that almost any organization can be won over to a spectrum of innovation. It requires management interventions on multiple fronts and tremendous determination on the part of intrapreneurs, managers, and leaders, but it can be done. Chapters 3–9 follow the strategic model I take into companies. They show that a Disrupt-It-Yourself approach has taken root in large and established organizations—and how this approach to innovation can be nurtured and sustained.

In aggregate, the takeaway across my model is this: get messy. The only way to change mind-sets and overcome the odds is to embrace the complexity of the organization and engage it on many fronts. Understand the pathology of the risk-averse, change-resistant, process-bound enterprise, and you begin to see the path forward.

THREE

Principle 1: Keep It Frugal

It may be the biggest debate to date in innovation circles: Does imposing constraints and leveraging ingenuity yield better results in the end? Or does it make more sense, if you care about innovation and want to see more attempts succeed, to show it a little more love, in the form of cash?

Intrapreneurs are famously resourceful. Many of the best stories about corporate innovation involve someone hacking a solution using limited resources, often in their spare time. I'm a huge fan of this approach, having coauthored a book full of them. (*Jugaad Innovation* took its name from the MacGyver-like frugal ingenuity practiced broadly in India, as in other emerging economies, and by entrepreneurs and increasingly by large firms in developed economies.[1]) But it's also true that most of the intrapreneurs I've known haven't exactly had the choice. They've either been working in situations where innovation was not in their job description and so no resources for exploration were available to them, or they were flying under the radar where they didn't want to access lavish resources before they were ready to reveal their findings. So did success come despite short funding or because of it? If someone has a promising idea in a company that prioritizes innovation, why not throw some money at him or her right away?

Tom and David Kelley of the design firm IDEO explain why not. "Although creative constraint sounds like an oxymoron," they wrote in *Creative Confidence*, "one way to spark creative action is to constrain it." They are quick to concede that "given a choice, most of us would of course prefer a little more budget, a little more staff, and a little more time." But they don't recommend loosening the purse strings: "Constraints can spur creativity and incite action, as long as you have the confidence to embrace them."[2] To confidence, I would add a flexible and asset-based mind-set. Importantly, these constraints help us do "less but better" in the words of *Essentialism: The Disciplined Pursuit of Less* author Greg McKeown. This approach is fundamental to the success of many intrapreneurs. McKeown reminds us that "*essentialism* is not about how to get more things done; it's about how to get the right things done."[3]

Creatives in the arts and entertainment world often lend support to this idea. Take the filmmaker Martin Villeneuve, who told a TED audience in 2013 about his experiences trying to make a sci-fi movie on a budget of $2 million. (Contrast this with, say, the 2013 Hollywood blockbuster *Iron Man 3*, budgeted at $200 million.) Granted, the critically acclaimed *Mars et Avril* took time and encountered numerous setbacks, but Villeneuve was convinced that "the more problems we had, the better the film got." He told the TED crowd: "If you treat the problems as possibilities, life will start to dance with you in the most amazing ways."[4] This plays out off the silver screen as well, even in highly regulated industries such as aerospace. For example, the entirety of India's Mangalyaan Mars mission cost just 4.5 billion rupees, or about $74 million. Compare this to NASA's own MAVEN Mars orbiter, which has a total mission cost of around $672 million—or, for that matter, the budget of *Gravity*, starring Sandra Bullock and George Clooney, which topped $100 million.

But others caution that starving your innovators is no way to produce a rich pipeline of new offerings.[5] Worse, it adds insult to injury, signaling to innovators that their efforts aren't valued.

Not surprisingly, this urgent question—fund or be frugal— comes up every day in my work with corporate clients and their disrupters. As part of that, I have developed *Disrupt-It-Yourself* as a concise playbook that puts frugal innovation into play in a way that benefits institutions and motivates innovators. It's a matter of understanding what works and why—and knowing what practices to abandon. Some of the best cases of ingenuity I've seen in my career reveal ways to unlock the power of frugal intrapreneurship to build a creative culture that keeps innovators engaged without breaking the bank.

Frugal Intrapreneurship in Situ

The story behind an ingenious product from Philips Healthcare raises questions about what innovation should cost, both to develop and for the customer to buy. A few years ago, the firm introduced an offering called Efficia ECG100. It was a low-cost, portable alternative to the expensive electrocardiogram (ECG) devices typically installed in hospitals for cardiac screening.

Ravi Ramaswamy, who led the innovation team behind it, says the impetus was a growing sense in the company that products for emerging markets should not simply be stripped-down versions of the solutions being sold in richer countries. They should be designed from the bottom up to fit a particular market's needs. In this case, there was also compelling personal interest from the team at the Philips Innovation Campus in Bangalore in designing medical devices for resource-constrained remote areas. They all knew people in both villages and urban areas who could benefit from them. Ramaswamy himself told a story of visiting a close friend who is a pediatrician in Thailand, and finding him in poor spirits: "He said that he lost two babies yesterday." Looking around the doctor's office, Ramaswamy couldn't believe what he was hearing: "Why did you lose them? You've got two incubators right over there." The friend shook his head. The equipment was "the best in the world," he agreed. "But my staff don't know how to use them. They are of no use to me." They were so complicated that local paramedics and nurses needed specialized training to use them. That's when Ramaswamy realized that anything he created for use in resource-constrained settings should not only be easy to buy but also easy to use.

The heart-monitoring solution that ended up meeting both criteria started with the team questioning the assumption that the two parts of an ECG—its data acquisition sensors and its data analysis and display capability—had to be together in the machine itself. In an age when smartphones are everywhere and people are familiar with their interfaces, the team figured it must be possible to use a mobile platform to create something highly portable, easy to use, and connected to a shared system located off-site. It would be capable of capturing, analyzing, and producing instant visualizations of that data.

Brilliant idea, right? But not obviously a major moneymaker for Philips. Ramaswamy knew he would need to make a great pitch to top management before asking for real resources. "I put together a team of eight or ten individuals," he told me, "and I stayed with them day and night." Right up front, he explained to his colleagues that this would be a labor of love. "This is something we have to do in our spare time," he said. "Let's do it over the weekend, in the evening—but at the same time, make sure that our daytime responsibilities do not suffer." Operating under the radar was temporary but necessary. On that basis, he challenged them: "Can we come up with a product prototype that will work?"

The prototype exceeded everyone's expectations. What is now a diagnostic-quality electrocardiogram started with the team's purchase of an off-the-shelf mobile device. Any Android phone or tablet could act as the user interface after the simple installation of an app. The team's energies went into making an ECG acquisition box that was just as compact (the final product weighed fewer than ten ounces) and intuitive to use. "We worked on it for about six to eight months," Ramaswamy recalled, before asking for a meeting with Philips Healthcare's business unit leader. After hearing the idea and trying out the prototype, the executive said: "This is a fantastic product. It's going to be the pathway to the future." Ramaswamy reported that "from then on, there was no looking back. We had the complete support of the business unit in terms of driving this model."

The enthusiastic response from the business unit leader suggests he might have recognized the Efficia ECG100 as the kind of *jugaad* innovation that can prove broadly transformative. Indeed, Ramaswamy notes about the redesigned cardiograph that "as we delve deeper into it, we also find relevance in the developed world . . . even the US." In richer markets, it may not be that hospitals would switch from more sophisticated to simpler equipment. Rather, the availability of this inexpensive, intuitive solution could allow for a dramatic expansion of the usage of ECG machines beyond the highly trained doctors who have been their sole users. This, along with its light weight and mobility, could upend existing assumptions about where and by whom health care can be delivered.

Now *that's* a success story. But would it have happened if the innovation team had gone down the typical product development path with full funding and executive oversight? Would it ever have seen the light of day? Ramaswamy barely blinks: *no way*.

THE SHIFT: KEEP IT FRUGAL

From	*To*
Placing few big bets	Including many small experiments and rapid prototyping
Defaulting to greater resources	Using fewer resources to bring more autonomy and spur creativity
Using complex and costly tools	Shifting to an asset-based mind-set, using simple/existing/off-the-shelf tools

Turning Old Assets into New Building Blocks

It's a great wrinkle in the Philips Healthcare story that the innovation itself was created for resource-poor customers. And it may be that innovating *for* high-value, low-cost scenarios helps teams embrace working *with* high-value, low-cost scenarios. But really these are different goals. One team can innovate luxury goods at very low cost, and another team can just as easily spend millions creating solutions for bottom-of-the-pyramid customers—and I've seen both being done by what are considered the world's most innovative companies. The takeaway from Philips is that producing high value at low cost requires being resourceful— which is a matter of skill but just as importantly a matter of mind-set. "For me, it is like looking at a glass half-full or a glass half-empty," Ramaswamy said. "I always like to look at it as half-full, and find ways and means of accomplishing a vision."

A classic way of describing what resourceful builders do is *bricolage*. The term comes from the French *bricoler* ("to tinker") and has a strong DIY connotation to it—people engaging in bricolage are using materials they have on hand to accomplish things they were never intended for. Looking at business settings, management scholars use the term to describe how intrapreneurs actively solve problems and seek opportunities, relying on preexisting elements and recombining resources for novel uses.[6] That's a perfect way to sum up, for example, how a frugal innovation initiative at the University of Queensland in Australia called the HyShot Flight Program managed to conduct the world's first successful test flight of a scramjet engine.

The idea of the scramjet—a supersonic jet that uses a very different propulsion system than conventional fuel combustion— was something NASA had already spent $100 million on, but as the university reported the news in 2001, the program led by its own Dr. Allan Paull had a budget of just $1.5 million. Its success "resulted from three years of scrounging and cobbling together of scientific and engineering partnerships" and plenty of goodwill from universities, governments, and scientists around the world. It also required some literal cobbling together. Paull explained: "Ours is a low-cost alternative, and we've had to develop all sorts of ancillary equipment on the cheap. We've bought a lot of bits and pieces off the shelf from automotive shops such as glues and silastics at $2 to $3 a pot." The press release issued by the university quipped that what Paull's team produced "may be a scrounge-jet, as well as a scramjet." But it concluded, "Financial adversity has inspired ingenuity."[7] Others, like Astro Teller of Alphabet's X R & D lab, agree: "If you're really trying to create a culture in which people run at the hardest parts of the problem first, that's not something in which people need a lot of money in order to be able to do. In fact, it's the opposite. The only people who can really afford to waste their money are people who have lots of money."[8]

David VanHimbergen is another industrious leader. He was CEO of Tide Spin, an on-demand laundry and dry-cleaning delivery service operating in the Chicago area. But only a few years ago he was just a Procter & Gamble (P&G) manager with an idea, looking around his organization for the means to make it a reality. The idea sprang from his observations about the consumer behavior of millennials, who "were starting to uncover savvy ways to outsource aspects of their life—things they're not invested in." Increasingly, he figured, one of those aspects would be doing laundry. He worked in a company that arguably knew more than anyone about how to sell detergent. How could they serve those consumers who wanted to outsource the task?

It wasn't long before Tide Spin was pursuing that line of reasoning, leveraging P&G's brand strength to make the business a preferred service provider. Based in Chicago, the Tide Spin team set up camp in a "coworking" space—a facility that opened in 2012 to allow digital startups to rent small amounts of office space and work side by side in a kind of entrepreneurial hothouse. As this tiny group went about figuring out a business model to make laundry pickup and delivery profitable for P&G, they used an off-the-shelf app at the onset, thereby stretching their bare-bones budget a little bit further and saving months of development time. The real breakthrough came when the team partnered with an existing asset within Procter & Gamble that it could leverage to save an enormous source of cost and risk: the Tide Dry Cleaning business which the company had started in 2008. With this service-model experiment already in place, the team saw a chance to piggyback on the physical facilities and thus be able to focus most of its thinking and resources on the customer experience.

Meanwhile, the team was tapping their networks across the sprawling organization for experience and advice on every aspect of the operation. VanHimbergen summed it up for me: "At a company the size of P&G, you can find an expert in just about any area. We have linguistics experts that are masters of text analytics. Why would you think we'd have that? But if you ask around, you find the right people."

Left and right the team was grabbing elements that were freely available—the Tide brand, the coworking space, the dry-cleaning shops, the app platforms, and the expert counsel. Rather than starting from scratch, they used existing assets differently to create something new and valuable.

The bricolage-style development I've been describing is something often associated with entrepreneurs; Phil Knight, for example, started Nike by teaming up with his former track coach and using a waffle iron to prototype the new sneaker sole they had in mind. But *intrapreneurs*, the disrupters inside of your organization, are also highly likely to operate in this fashion because they are inside companies with numerous underutilized resources around them just waiting to be repurposed.

This bricolage/DIY ideal of intrapreneurship outlines a clear path for frugal innovation. But before we pull all the loose ends together, let's inspect the one thing that can throw motivated innovators off the scent of invention almost immediately: funding.

The High Cost of Spending Money

The fact that intrapreneurs can do impactful things with limited funds doesn't mean that they can't find ways to spend money if they have it. There are so many ways to push resources into innovation projects that, theoretically, any idea could have any amount allocated to it—and the team could easily use it up. I often run an interactive exercise with clients where we divide the group into two teams. Each team has the same problem to solve—but one team gets a $100 budget while the other gets $1 million. Invariably, the $1 million team finds a way to spend its money—whether or not it's needed. Why? One, it's human nature, and two, they're trained that way. In most organizations, if you don't spend your budget this year, you lose it next year. But most cases of this type of spending, even in real scenarios, turns out to be discretionary. It's simple: when we have the budget, we reach outside the company's walls to consultants, contractors, and solution providers rather than leveraging the resources we already have, including ingenuity, knowledge, and networks, to figure out the problem.

In a recent discussion thread on the question-and-answer website Quora, someone asked what it would typically cost to engage an industrial design firm. One respondent, Sam

Birchenough, is the owner of a product design and development firm in Los Angeles, which he describes as smaller than midsized firms like IDEO, but very capable. "I'll tell you one thing," he began. "As a design firm, we quote far less than larger firms [but] most potential clients are still shocked at the actual cost-to-market of their idea. I gave a rough quote of ~$40k just today to design, engineer, and prototype a small electronic wearable device (excluding pcb design and software)."[9] Birchenough found that "this was a much[,] much higher number than the person was expecting," but his point was that others would see it as chump change. With consultants in other firms billing out at anywhere from $150 to $500 per hour, depending on the kind of work being done, $40,000 might get you a three-person team working on your problem for all of one week. Or more likely, it would not get you even that, because the consultancy would not bother taking on such a small project. Ben Einstein, a venture capitalist who provides advice and mentoring to his seed-stage founders, wrote that even if you've just received a significant amount of funding, "hiring a design firm is plain old expensive . . . It's not uncommon for functional prototypes to cost $500K for a full development cycle."[10]

Often, an intrapreneurial team is able to avoid nearly every kind of cost, assuming it has the time, the access, and the relationships to tap into internal expertise. The irony is that when big budgets are allocated to internal ventures, it's not always because the project is known to *need* a lot of funding but because management is using budget as a signaling device. To constituencies both inside and outside the company, major investment says, "This is important." And it's true; that can be self-fulfilling. After all, if a project isn't expensive, top management may feel very little responsibility for whether it succeeds. By allocating major funds, executives force themselves to keep paying attention. Of course, more resources also make it easier to attract capable leadership and other talent to a project, as then it seems like something the company is committed to.

But there are other ways to get buy-in without spending eye-popping sums of money. This is what I saw at Pernod Ricard. Amandine Robin told me about some internal innovations she and the other eight members of the company's first "Youth Action Council" (YAC) hatched. One, for example, is an Airbnb-style site called HomeViviality, which is an insider home-borrowing option for Pernod Ricard people on the road. Amandine said the YAC was determined to proceed frugally: "In all of our initiatives, we wanted to have the entrepreneur mind-set—meaning it's self-funding and it's not a huge budget." Every problem that came up, they tried to solve "as an entrepreneur would, who generally doesn't have lots of money but has lots of creativity." Despite their low-budget profile, the group had a high profile in terms of visibility and access to top management, because YAC was specially commissioned by the CEO, housed in a work area near the C-suite, and had a standing slot on the agenda of periodic executive meetings and offsites.

BARRIERS TO KEEPING IT FRUGAL

- Less funding = less oversight
- It can feel risky
- No template or established metrics: harder to measure progress
- Requires identification of nonfinancial support: time + assets

Amandine may be a little like the intrapreneurs in your organization. They might choose to forgo formal funding in exchange for flying under the radar. Why? Because they know that keeping it frugal is the best chance they have to succeed.

A Different Type of Innovator's Dilemma

Throwing money around like a rock star is never a responsible thing for an enterprise to do. But the bigger issue with early-stage projects is that spending a lot on them can actually damage their chances for success. I'm not talking about the effects of constraints on sheer creativity, where the jury may still be out. Beyond the inventiveness of the ideas themselves, I'm talking about the organizational dynamics that kick into gear when a large budget is allocated.

Simply stated, when you spend more on a project than is required to produce a given amount of value, your ROI—both your return on investment and return on intelligence, as we'll talk about in chapter 7—goes down. This means the initiative operates longer in the red, making it more vulnerable each day to someone asking, "Couldn't we find better uses for these resources?" One great advantage of an innovation produced on a tiny budget is that if it succeeds at all, it offers instant positive ROI.

Because well-resourced projects invite more scrutiny, they are subject to more interference. Multiple cooks start showing up in the kitchen, adding their own seasoning to the broth. And projects with a sizable budget are typically housed within an existing business unit—one that has its established business model and procedures, and that unit immediately starts to set the project team straight on how things are supposed to be done and what matters most.

So intrapreneurs operate more efficiently sans the official oversight that comes with a big budget. Without it, intrapreneurs can retain the creative control they want longer—staying closely connected to customer needs, whether or not they fit neatly into an existing business model. Ravi Ramaswamy was very cognizant that he needed to keep the cost of his efforts down: "At some point, we got funded for it. And I said, 'We should keep it below the cost of other things,' because I knew that the business unit would come after me saying, 'Why are you wasting time and money when we already have a product [like this]?'"

In some ways it is worse when a project manages to win over many hearts and minds in the organization at too early a point. As an innovative idea visibly starts to gain traction, increasing numbers of people are drawn to it and want a piece of it. It can feel great to have that affirmation, but these are often not the kinds of contributors a startup needs. Some are there for the intrinsic rewards; others only find it appealing once it offers extrinsic ones. Neil Tambe, who started at Deloitte Consulting and now hones his intrapreneurial skills in a government role in Detroit, made this point well. In a post on his blog, Tambe warned executives not to go out of their way to convince skeptics to sign on to innovation teams, especially by sugarcoating the process or perks. Instead, he advised: "Tell people the truth and find people who are passionate about what you're doing." In his experience, "those passionate people are the ones who stick with you through thick and thin"—mainly because "they care about making an impact, not what they'll get out of joining your team."[11]

People who are really passionate about their ideas will forge ahead even if they don't have the so-called appropriate resources or the time allotted; the corollary is that in settings with ample resources, projects will go ahead that *don't* have that same amount of passion attached to them. But ultimately it is the passion and purpose, not the resources, that drive success (a subject we will return to in chapter 9). So the lack of resources can have the pleasant side effect of shaking out the "meh" projects.

This is exactly why Babak Forutanpour at Qualcomm turned down the offer of resources and just asked for pizza money. Keeping it frugal becomes a no-brainer—and it's second nature to intrapreneurs.

The DIY Playbook—Keep It Frugal

All the evidence above demonstrates that it is getting easier for organizations to invent their future little by little at a very low cost. This isn't the case only for intrapreneurs—it's easier for everyone. This is considered a fact in the startup world. When I asked Salim Ismail for his take, he nodded, saying, "Innovation once cost a lot, and now it does not." I couldn't agree more.

What organizations need now are the right tools and a ready mind-set to innovate from within. The Disrupt-It-Yourself agenda items that follow directly support my main message: deep-six the deep pockets. Simple tools, small budgets, and human ingenuity can deliver impressive results, including maximum agility with fewer "business as usual" strings attached.

Together with the plays contained in chapters 4–9, these action items are designed to give you a fast, flexible way to create a disruptive culture. Knowing that nothing innovative is ever truly linear (or one size fits all), consider these to be á la carte strategies for keeping it frugal:

1. Remain Asset-Based
2. Keep It Simple
3. Encourage Frugal Experiments
4. Focus on Teams
5. Rethink Incentives

1. Remain Asset-Based

Recycle resources. At Pernod Ricard, intrapreneurs told me about the "circular economy" that exists within their production facilities, meaning nothing gets lost and resources such as ingredients are reused along the production chain. Constructive disrupters have an asset-based mind-set that enables them to reuse existing resources, repurpose hardware, ask around internally for coaching and expertise, hack their own solutions, and scrounge for parts to cobble together prototypes.

Share infrastructure. In addition to reusing internal resources, intrapreneurs can tap into the same third-party infrastructure as entrepreneurs. They can get web services through pay-by-the-sip vendors like Amazon; they can go to 3D printing shops to produce hardware prototypes; they can install themselves in coworking spaces just as the Tide Spin team did.

Create a frugal culture. The play for organizations is to create a culture where it's okay to use duct tape and discarded material for experiments—both literally and figuratively. Even more, people from across the organization need to be ready and willing to share their specialized knowledge and expertise. Increasingly, managers in big corporations need to focus on frugal execution and to identify, hire, and retain the people they find to be most resourceful through interviews, recommendations, and past history of frugal experimentation.

2. Keep It Simple

Skip the extras. In an agile software environment, simplicity is about maximizing the work not done. Likewise, simplicity is a hallmark of frugal intrapreneurship. Too many bows and bells rob resources and add sparse value, especially in the early stages of development. The team at Philips Healthcare put this into play perfectly with their high-value, low-cost ECG device: it's portable, practical, and devoid of extraneous features.

Target value. As you mix simplicity into your organizational mantra, keep your design approach simple and focus on value first. Doing less with fewer steps is more effective when actions are orchestrated to target only the critical benefits you know you need.

Focus on customer needs. The top intrapreneurs in your shop are usually sitting close to the front line, or otherwise have direct access to what customers want right now, or know about a pain that has yet to be addressed. Listen to these folks, take their ideas to heart, and help create a pathway to execution.

Make autonomy a top priority. Simplicity needs to filter across to organizational design. With fewer layers of accountability, innovators can stay "stealth" and remain free from attack by the natural immune system of the organization.

3. Encourage Frugal Experiments

Enable side projects. It used to be that R&D experimentation was a high-stakes game. You were betting a chunk of capital on success, so failure wasn't an option. Today, frugal experimentation makes it possible to have a portfolio of small, diverse bets off the books that nobody even knows about. Remember Balanda Atis from L'Oréal? She and a few like-minded colleagues conducted experiments on the side that eventually contributed to a new blockbuster product line.

Make small bets. Small-scale experiments make it feasible to fly under the radar and test multiple ideas at once. Then, when something takes off, you can double down without hand-wringing about leaving other experiments behind. This approach allows for quick returns while mitigating risk.

Leverage early wins. Build on small victories to gain momentum. Tide Spin's VanHimbergen acknowledged that the venture was "messy for the first six or so months" and required trial and error to nail down the business model. Their early win came when they partnered with the Tide Dry Cleaners franchise—a P&G startup running under its own set of rules. It freed up their micro operating budget and allowed them to invest in the new staff they needed to scale the venture.[12]

Actually build something. Product prototypes (or minimum viable products) create a path for validation and development. As we've seen, it's plausible to cobble together prototypes with sparse funding, using asset-based thinking, and come up with something tangible to guide iteration. One intrapreneur put it this way: "Anything can sound good on paper, but by the time the prototype is developed, I have a team of collaborators who are knowledgeable and passionate enough to sell the idea to executives. And stakeholders have something tangible to look at and pass around." Ramaswamy concurred: "You can talk about a possible product, but it's a very different feeling when you can put a prototype on the table and start touching it to see how the machine responds to your needs."

And the kicker: When the Philips ECG machine was finally integrated into a product line, much of the groundwork for manufacturing and distribution was already laid out across the organization by the intrapreneurs who had built the prototype and the colleagues they enlisted along the way. *Boom*: That's what "keep it frugal" looks like.

4. Focus on Teams

Create quality teams. This new reality—that "innovation once cost a lot, and now it does not," to quote Ismail—is why organizations need to focus on creating quality teams over choosing any specific early-stage concept. The assumption is not only that the idea will likely need to pivot but that some teams are more capable than others of pivoting—plus those teams can make quick progress because putting together a minimum viable product to test is so inexpensive.

Look for passion. How do you know a great team when you see one? I put my money on passion, ingenuity, and agility as leading indicators of success. Intrapreneurs are enabled by technology—but they are motivated by a shared passion to solve a problem.

5. Rethink Incentives

Experiment with incentives. There's an ongoing question of frugality (or generosity) as it relates to individuals' compensation—in other words, how much financial reward should go to the innovators? Some companies put forward personal or intangible rewards that are appealing but not all that expensive. At Stanley Black & Decker, for example, the inducement to enter one of its innovation competitions is the chance to drive the company-owned Tesla for a month. While that may kick-start the motivation of many, it might not be quite enough for some. The firm also provides time with senior leadership or a chance to share learnings with their colleagues on a broad platform. I wholeheartedly agree with Ismail, who says that incentives should go to the point of giving intrapreneurs real "upside" potential—that is, an actual stake in the ultimate market success of the innovation. The bottom line is that organizations need to experiment with incentives and decide for themselves what works within their walls.

Use respect as remuneration. It's critical to create compensation that syncs with the "keep it frugal" ethos. What I know for sure is that companies absolutely must deliver psychic rewards such as trust and respect. Intrapreneurs should be celebrated. They should be given the opportunity to take the ball and run with it, to lead the initiative and take it to scale. That is the type of incentive that motivates the passionate problem solvers that step up and become intrapreneurs. This is all about autonomy. Daniel H. Pink, the best-selling author of *Drive: The Surprising Truth About What Motivates Us*, argued convincingly that mastery, autonomy, and purpose are the three big motivators of human achievement—and some of his favorite examples were intrapreneurs.[13]

Executive Scorecard

- Do you model the "keep it frugal" ethos in a positive way to maximize intrapreneurship?
- Have you created a culture where people share infrastructure and reuse resources for intrapreneurial ventures?
- Do you take value and customer focus seriously in innovative efforts?
- Are simplicity and autonomy a part of your organization?
- Do you experiment with nonfinancial incentives for intrapreneurs?

FOUR

Principle 2: Make It Permissionless

Grace Hopper, the mathematician and US naval officer behind the first computer compiler, was known for her programming creativity and also for having a way with words. Hopper had a lot of ideas that challenged convention—including that programming languages should be machine-independent (that one led to the development of the programming language COBOL)—and she also encouraged the people around her to do more boundary pushing. You might not recognize her name, but you've probably heard the famous expression attributed to her: "It's easier to ask forgiveness than it is to get permission."[1]

That sentiment is a common thread that cuts across the experience of successful intrapreneurs. In fact, it is arguably a pillar of intrapreneurship everywhere. Take the wholesale redevelopment of the 2013 Toyota Avalon. Led by designers and engineers working far from the company's Japanese headquarters, the initiative was culture defying for Toyota. When the US-based team told their story to industry analyst Mark Phelan, they stressed that they "worked in the margins of Toyota's playbook, following the old adage that it's better to beg forgiveness than permission."[2] I also heard the phrase from Marc Nager, founder of Startup Weekend and managing director at Telluride Venture Accelerator. He said that companies need a "culture of permissionless innovation," and "innovation isn't something that you should be asking approval for. You shouldn't have to sell to your boss." And when Alexis Ohanian wrote an entrepreneurial memoir of how he and Steve Huffman created the social news aggregation site Reddit.com, he aptly titled it *Without Their Permission*.[3]

Having worked with a lot of innovators, I've seen that they aren't trying to be defiant exactly—especially the ones who work within large enterprises. Intrapreneurs aren't breaking rules for the sheer thrill of it. They simply want to get something done that they suspect will be derailed by bureaucracy if they ask for permission to proceed. So they get really good at sidestepping, bypassing, and ducking conversations in which they would likely be told no or "go back to your day job." Their plan is to take an idea far enough so that when it is ultimately unveiled to decision makers in the organization, it will be far too valuable to refuse or shut down.

Perhaps like you, I find myself celebrating the underdog instincts and clever end runs that ultimately lead to breakthrough accomplishments for innovators and their organizations. After all, against-all-odds, eleventh-hour success is inspiring. At the same time, is it really effective for employers to settle for a surreptitious approach to something as important as intra-preneurship? Enterprises whose leaders are focused on internal innovation and organic growth, such as Intuit and Amazon, are finding more deliberate ways to legitimize and support experi-mentation. In fact, organizations can learn a lot from what I see as a slightly different version of "making it permissionless."

Let's examine what *permissionless* looks like today in organi-zations before considering a new model that lets leaders provide support without crushing the creativity and potential of upstart intrapreneurs.

The Look and Feel of Permission-Free: Flying the Pirate Flag

Intrapreneurs have several stealth strategies they adopt to route around all these bothersome permission issues. They do end runs, fly under the radar, go rogue, and even engage in hacking behavior.

In some organizations, intrapreneurs resort to what innovation consultant Thomas Wedell-Wedellsborg calls "stealthstorming." In an article for *Forbes*, he told the story of an innovation within Pfizer (called pfizerWorks), dreamed up by Jordan Cohen, a manager in its HR department. As Cohen looked across the entire company, he saw legions of knowledge workers who were frustrated spending time on mundane tasks when there were so many more creative things they could be doing. He designed pfizerWorks to be an internal temp service of sorts, staffed with people who were vetted and trained on enterprise systems and who were available around the clock at a standard fair price to anyone who had the funds in their budgets to spend. Brilliant!

Cohen got pretty far providing this service internally without having to explain it to anyone with the power to shut it down.[4] But as it scaled up and required more of his time, he "couldn't continue to pretend the project didn't exist." This is where some deliberate concealment kicked in. "To deflect questions, Cohen told people it was part of a companywide initiative called Adapting to Scale (ATS), which was aimed at standardizing processes and sharing best practices. Nobody knew exactly what ATS involved—and pfizerWorks *was* in fact aligned with the initiative—so Cohen's story provided adequate cover, allowing him to spend time on pfizerWorks for a time without raising awkward questions."[5] He saw it as deflection for the greater good.

A less subversive tactic for avoiding permission is "running at the resistance" to try to defuse it—like an end run. Dipanjan Chatterjee, lead strategist at Target, wields this tactic as a way to beat naysayers to the punch: he identifies the risks of a project himself at the outset and tries to neutralize them early on rather than ducking them later. At Lowe's, the building products retailer, Kyle Nel, shared a similar strategy for clearing a path through the bureaucratic thicket there: "My biggest advocates were in the legal and risk mitigation areas. This is largely because I enlisted them early." Both Chatterjee and Nel are being proactive rather than deceptive.

If you really want to see inventive individuals subverting formal authority, go into a government setting. Mitchell Weiss studies "public entrepreneurship" and the intrapreneurial activity that happens within federal agencies and nongovernmental organizations (NGOs). In that realm, he says "hacking the bureaucracy" is a term that is increasingly used. "Bureaucratic hacks adhere to the law but make use of little-known or little-used provisions to get things done faster," he explained. The obvious analogy is hacking an information system by finding a bug to exploit. He has seen public employees take this approach to hire new tech workers and speed website releases, for example. "I recently spoke with a big-city procurement officer who was lamenting his inability to run pilot programs," Weiss reported. At the suggestion that maybe there was some hackable bug in the policy code, the officer decided to look it up and study the fine print. Sure enough, "buried in it was the very permission he was looking for."[6]

BARRIERS TO MAKING IT PERMISSIONLESS

- For managers, granting permission to innovate takes time away from core business activities.
- Fear and uncertainty prevent action—it requires trust.
- It means saying yes more often.
- It's culturally unacceptable—middle managers and others may balk.

When I asked Bob Schwartz of GE Healthcare how he managed the permission process, he essentially said, "*We didn't.*" "We were subversive. We didn't ask anyone's permission," he said. To Schwartz, "every single thing that requires intrapreneurship is something that's off the grid and under the radar."

Subversive or not, permission is sometimes out of the question logistically. Sometimes just identifying the decision maker can be difficult, let alone gaining access to that person. At times, the intrapreneur's idea relates to a different part of the enterprise, or no one in the chain of command "owns" the problem it would solve. Or maybe it falls between, falls outside, or cuts across organizational lines in a way that makes it unclear "who has the D" (to use Paul Rogers's and Marcia Blenko's phrase).[7]

Regardless of the strategy or rationale, most intrapreneurs seem to believe that this is just how it needs to be. The system around them is impenetrable and built for a purpose that never anticipated what they are trying to do. Unfortunately, all this unilateral innovation eventually creates difficulties for intrapreneurs as well as organizations.

When Permissionless Is a Problem: Part 1

For intrapreneurs, going stealth loses its utility when they eventually need management's blessing. Sometimes this occurs when customer feedback is required to take an idea to the next level. (It can be hard to reach out to real customers when customer relationships are closely held by those who "own" them.) Other times entrepreneurs need to bring managers into the loop because a more substantial investment, and perhaps additional knowledge, is required. As we saw in chapter 3, a lot can be accomplished on a very frugal basis, but there comes a time when a team needs expertise it doesn't have or funds to cover expenses that can't be paid with slack in an operations budget.

In other situations, intrapreneurs need to get on management's radar because their industry context is especially rules-based. For example, there may be risks of running afoul of industry regulations. In sectors such as finance and health care, it doesn't take much deviation from the status quo to get into fraught legal territory. There's a reason that at Citigroup, experiments in areas including blockchain distributed ledger technologies and cryptocurrencies are happening under the direction of the formal Citi Innovation Labs. In banking, things have to be done by the book, and *rogue* is not exactly a term of endearment. For that matter, most industries are subject to some type of regulation.

Intrapreneurs eventually need to come in from the cold. Proceeding without permission is really just a question of getting things underway—getting into action, with the intent of asking for forgiveness when the odds are very good it will be granted.

When Permissionless Is a Problem: Part 2

Underground innovation is no walk in the park for bosses either. As soon as a manager or senior leader becomes officially aware of a project, she must react, either by accepting responsibility for it or killing it. It is now being pursued on her watch. At the very least she must become informed about it and prepared to explain it to her own higher-ups.

All of this puts a lot of pressure on management. When stealth innovators come clean, they're essentially asking someone else to take on some reputational risk, but it's likely someone who doesn't share their passion for the idea and won't get much credit if it succeeds. This is the kind of situation where Patrick Doyle, former CEO of Domino's Pizza, talks about "omission bias" creeping into a manager's thinking. His point is that managers are more worried about being responsible for "sins of commission" (mismanaging a task that is clearly expected of them) than about their "sins of omission" (neglecting to pursue or support a new idea).[8] Certainly careers suffer more from managers' visible actions than from their invisible inactions, even if the two are equally damaging to the company's future.

The second problem managers face is that any deviation from the status quo represents some level of business risk. Chatterjee readies himself for this barrier when he finds himself in front of a senior group to get buy-in for a new way of working. "They just love saying, 'Well, this is a great idea but . . .'—*boom*—'have you thought about *this* risk?'" Yet Chatterjee can't blame organizations for balking at being blindsided. Ultimately, it's management's job to find and mitigate risk. Without some of that, there would be no business to innovate. Again, someone who is just coming into the loop is seldom fired up with passion for an idea, and they are more likely to see the legitimate downside.

The third problem managers face is losing their best and brightest people because they are not in a position to support them as they would like. Plenty of research, going back a long way, has established that innovation-minded employees tend to leave companies when their ideas don't gain traction. Rosabeth Moss Kanter found more than a quarter century ago that if intrapreneurs perceive their organizations to be too bureaucratic to change, they are likely to decamp.[9]

This is why some managers turn a blind eye to rogue endeavors. The rule-benders get away with their covert work because, on some level, their bosses know that it's valuable. And sometimes they would rather not be forced to take an official stand on stealth projects. They are supportive of what's going on—as long as they don't have to go on the record about it.

All of this leads to ambiguity, and on both sides: Managers, on the one hand, don't want to crush intrapreneurial efforts, so they live by an ineffectual "see no evil/hear no evil" philosophy. Intrapreneurs, on the other hand, are afraid of being shut down, so at times they keep things under wraps longer than they should. How can intrapreneurs and organizations mitigate this ambiguity together? We'll look at some best practices and then move on to a permissionless playbook that applies to all organizations.

THE SHIFT: MAKE IT PERMISSIONLESS

From	To
Complex and multilayered approval system	Fast, nimble, and low-friction approval process
Centralized innovation approach	Decentralized approach—innovation across the organization and at the edge
Leadership that micromanages and confines	Leadership that is deeply trusting, provides "air cover," and creates space for intrapreneurs

Give Permission—to Skip Permission

Intuit, maker of TurboTax and QuickBooks, has thought a lot about the tension I'm emphasizing and has come up with some smart ways to resolve it.

Jeff Zias, who leads the company's "unstructured time" provision, explained to me why this specific idea is part of a larger solution at Intuit. "What's different and fundamental for us is that in our case, with about eight thousand employees, we want everybody to feel empowered to innovate, and in fact feel *required* to some degree to innovate."

By "unstructured time," Zias is referring to what many of us have learned to call 15 or 20 percent time. Like some other companies, starting with 3M (back in 1948), Intuit encourages employees to use a percentage of their on-the-clock time to develop relevant side projects. At Google, for example, 20 percent time was credited with giving employees the latitude to develop ideas that turned into Gmail and AdSense. Yet Google's own experience—it shut down its 20 percent policy in 2013—suggests that it isn't enough to just announce that people can and should spend the equivalent of a day a week on passion projects. According to Zias, Intuit realized it needed to do more to "inject some structure into that unstructured time."

One way the company does this is by hosting periodic multiday "hackathons," where teams of developers present pet projects and compete to tackle specific challenges aligned with the company's broader strategy (for example: easy, fast tax-return completion) in exchange for prizes and recognition. The cloud storage company Dropbox does something very similar in its "Hack Week," which one of its managers described as "an entire five days every summer for people to explore whatever projects interest them." Dropbox doesn't insist that the projects be aligned with any themes, but "what's really great," he said, "is that people end up working on projects that deeply benefit Dropbox in some way or another." Hack Week is therefore "the celebration of, *yeah*, you should be able to have an idea and own it and see it all the way through."[10]

But intrapreneurs at Intuit are not left to sink or swim on their own. The company supports project sponsors through multiple stakeholders. First, they have people whose whole job is coaching and encouraging innovation (Zias is one of them). Next, the organization's innovation catalysts are trained volunteers who spend 10 percent of their time guiding other employees to use design principles to create products that improve customers' lives. Finally, managers across Intuit are expressly incentivized to recognize and support entrepreneurial behavior and experimentation.

Intuit's approach is to leave intrapreneurs in that mode of "not asking permission" but giving them a legitimate structure for operating that way.

Offer the "Institutional Yes"

Giving people formal license to proceed without permission, as Intuit does, is one way to decriminalize proactive innovation. Another approach is what Jeff Bezos calls "the institutional yes"—a reflexive response on the part of managers to greenlight experiments in innovation rather than hit the brakes on them.

As part of that, Amazon has a setup called "working backwards," which begins with innovators drawing up press releases and FAQ documents for their early-stage ideas—as though they have become reality and it's launch day. Teams are encouraged to do this as a first step with any idea they hope ultimately to get funded, and to immediately start floating it with possible sponsors.

This is the opposite of keeping projects under wraps till they are ready for prime time. This puts an idea front and center almost as soon as it pops into someone's mind. Amazon works this way because it wants things out in the open, where they can be encouraged and honed with multiple perspectives—and where the rest of the organization can learn from them. (We'll get into this point more deeply in chapter 7's discussion of return on intelligence.) But to achieve this, Amazon needs to make sure intrapreneurial ideas don't perish on first contact with the cruel managerial world. That means keeping positional authority in check and giving people at all levels the ability to greenlight experiments.

Jeff Wilke, Amazon's chief executive of worldwide consumer, told *Forbes*: "We set up an environment where basically anyone can say 'yes' as long as they have the resources to begin to support it."[11] Along with that empowerment goes a lot of training to overcome the knee-jerk response to risk.

Another concept Bezos shares with decision makers across Amazon is the difference between "one-way doors" and "two-way doors." If a decision forces you to walk through a one-way door, that means there is no going back. You must continue down that path. Most decisions, however, are two-way doors: you can step across the threshold, and if you don't like what you see, you can turn around with minimal expenditure lost and some valuable lessons learned. Amazon constantly reminds managers, as they're looking at innovation ideas, not to mistake two-way doors for one-way doors. The upshot is they'll say yes more often.

There is much more to Amazon's approach to putting internal innovation on rails and turning into an "invention machine." For me, it all fits under the general philosophy of up-front permission granting: as long as you're taking smart risks, innovation means never having to say you're sorry.

Provide Air Cover

Cristina Notermann, director of product insights at the retail giant Target, brings forward and supports many intrapreneurial efforts. When I asked her about the most important thing for translating ideas to impact, she didn't hesitate. "Number one: we need leadership to provide air cover." This is something I heard in several of my interviews and recognize as a main way to avoid the "permissionless" conundrum. Providing air cover—having someone at a high level serving as your defender—is effectively granting permission to break a few rules. It means when someone at an intermediate level calls you out for your breach of protocol, you have a powerful champion to protect you from the consequences.

In companies across sectors, from Fidelity to Target to

Philips, I've consistently seen innovations that owe their existence to air cover from managers and executives alike.

At Pernod Ricard, it was the CEO who set up an intrapreneurial group and gave them "carte blanche," in the words of Amandine Robin. Then, to make sure it wasn't *only* the CEO providing air cover, she and the other members of the Youth Action Council got onstage at a management meeting of global unit CEOs. Robin told me: "We introduced what we wanted to do and told them that we might have ideas that are outside of the box, ideas that you might think are a bit crazy. 'All that we ask of you, our CEOs around the world, is to be open to the ideas that we bring.' We actually asked them to say yes, and they all screamed, 'Yes!'"

Air cover is an idea that resonated with USAID's Seema Patel as well. She said: "Air cover in government can come from lots of different places, not just your own senior leadership. Say the White House puts out a memo about open government and encourages all federal agencies to think about how they engage citizens in innovation. That's air cover."

Air cover, the institutional yes, and permission to skip permission all create the space and autonomy intrapreneurs need to flourish. These ideas, plus the strategies in the Disrupt-It-Yourself playbook below, are designed to keep your most creative people engaged in forging the future of the company.

The DIY Playbook—Make It Permissionless

Making intrapreneurship sustainable requires creating a permission-lite environment for intrapreneurs. It's autonomy with guardrails. The goal is to establish a network of support rather than a system of tight control by leaders. This "support, don't control" mantra reinforces frugal funding and has two additional benefits. First, it is an easy fit for intrapreneurs, who want a safe space to pursue new ideas and side projects. Second, it doesn't oblige large companies and their leaders to bend over backward to manage and measure early-stage projects. Here are the plays that put permissionless to work:

1. Support, Don't Control
2. Say Yes More Often
3. Add Light Structure

1. Support, Don't Control

Provide air cover. Intrapreneurs need support from senior leaders. We saw companies such as Pernod Ricard and USAID providing high-level air cover to promising initiatives that would otherwise be under assault from corporate antibodies that kill intrapreneurship.

Mentor, don't control. Support innovators with coaching, mentoring, and training. This type of reinforcement gives them low-cost assistance and keeps eyes on their efforts without choking off the ingenuity and creative magic that comes with the intrapreneurial process.

Listen up. Part of granting permission is stopping to listen to intrapreneurial ideas instead of nixing them off the bat based on risks or logistics—or the big killer, the business-as-usual process. We know that Amazon puts this play to good use. A software engineer named Charlie Ward, for example, planted the seed of Amazon Prime when he made an employee suggestion to offer free shipping.[12] And Alexa, the voice of the company's popular Echo devices, grew out of an internal team's proposal for an "intelligent personal assistant."[13]

2. Say Yes More Often

Create a permissionless culture. Companies like Amazon are known for granting permission for experimentation. Take their lead and try to create a more permission-granting culture by instituting a policy called the institutional yes. This and similar moves make it hard to say no so that people can reveal their ideas without expecting to be blocked.

Make permissionless the rule, rather than the exception. Decide on the degree to which permissionless will work for you, and build it into your business. Intuit's approach is to make some amount of "not asking permission" accepted and expected rather than a shady thing. Essentially, it has put in place features that allow intrapreneurs to accomplish quite a bit before they take the lid off whatever they've been cooking up.

Let their pirate flag fly. Some intrapreneurs draw energy from being able to see themselves as the rebels and pirates who are ready to defy the rules and risk censure to realize their visions. Companies need to manage the balance: If you treat intrapreneurship as a criminal offense, you'll get too little of it. But if you make it too law-abiding, you might just kill it off even faster.

Make it okay to pull the plug. Intrapreneurs should make the call about when to self-correct, pivot, or end a pilot or experiment. This level of autonomy creates trust, preserves passion, and encourages intrapreneurs to use what they learn to discover a more feasible solution.

3. Add Light Structure

Create permissionless programs. Design your own program to give employees permission to innovate within established parameters. Consider the innovation challenges and competitive hackathons that many companies launch internally. Some of these are inspired by highly visible open contests like the $10 million Ansari X PRIZE, which challenged comers to develop a spacecraft capable of entering space and returning safely twice within ten days. Elon Musk's Hyperloop-related challenges are another high-profile example. Companies that replicate this kind of thing within their own walls can often point to exciting results. At Facebook, for example, the "like" button came out of such a process.[14]

Fund free time. An alternative to Intuit's unstructured time is unstructured money. Adobe, for one, gives intrapreneurs a stipend to get them started. Through what it calls its "Kickbox" initiative (involving red boxes around the building with kickstarter kits for innovators), it gives any employee who agrees to participate in a two-day innovation workshop a prepaid credit card with $1,000 loaded on it. With that money, they are challenged to bring the idea as far into prototype territory as they can, at which point they make a pitch to win funding at a more generous level.[15] In other words, Adobe not only gives permission; it also provides light structure and frugal funding.

Choose one rule. Few organizations can eliminate permission altogether. Instead, try choosing one solid guardrail and launch from there. "Innovate within your job area" or "keep side projects simple" or "spend time but not money" are all one-rule ideas to try if you want to land on the side of permissionless innovation.

Extend permissionless to customers. Few organizations offer a permissionless path to enroll customers in intrapreneurial trials. Yet customer feedback is a key component for validating (or shutting down) ideas. Intuit broke down this particular barrier by giving employees permission to create a prototype and test their hypothesis with *just one customer*. And not just any customer, but one who is hypothesized to be well served by the solution. If that single customer uses the solution and recommends it to others, then the intrapreneur is encouraged to scale it up to a larger cohort of customers in order to collect more data.

Executive Scorecard

- What level of permissionless intrapreneurship can you live with, and how will you formalize it in your organization?
- How much air cover do you provide for intrapreneurs to make your environment a safe place to innovate?
- Is intrapreneurship occurring perpetually below the radar in your organization because you do not have the proper supports in place to enable it to bubble up?
- Does your culture allow leaders to listen to intrapreneurial ideas—and say yes more often?
- What programs do you have in place that add guardrails and structure, allowing innovators to proceed without formal permission?
- Do you provide support, training, and mentoring for intrapreneurs without imposing strict control over project decisions?

FIVE

Principle 3: Let Customers Lead

At an office of the giant business software company SAP in Calgary, Canada, Wayne Morris served as program director for service innovation, part of a global team whose focus is on speeding up the firm's applications of emerging technologies. One story he shared with me shows just how much acceleration can happen when the right connections are made.

Some years ago, he was meeting with one of SAP's large business customers and touting an innovative software application the firm had just released. The customer got the point of it immediately, but wasn't sure it quite hit the mark. As Morris recalls, the customer said, "Well, here's where I think you have a gap," and he went on to describe the functionality his department could really use. Shortly afterward, when Morris found himself in the development team's building and stopped by to tell them about the customer's wish, he got a pleasant surprise. They said, "You mean something like *this?*" As it happened, two developers on a different team had been working on that very problem for the past year as a pet project and had a solution that was more than half-baked. "Spot-on," Morris told them. "That's *exactly* what would fill the gap." It was given priority status for development and incorporated into the very next release of the product—which obviously satisfied the customer but also delighted the developers. "They felt incredibly happy that finally someone had acknowledged the work that they'd done," Morris said, "and they could be very proud that their invention had become part of a product and now could be called an innovation."

Nothing clears the way for intrapreneurship like the ability to connect with real customers' pressing needs. But could it be less left to chance? Consider the next words out of Morris's mouth: "We didn't have a way of surfacing something like that in the past." Therefore, the connection he made that week was a random, lucky event: "I happened to have a visit scheduled and they showed it to me. It was lucky." I would argue, as Morris did, for shifting that kind of connection from being a purely serendipitous event to a purposeful, supported endeavor. Responsible access to customers is the biggest thing managers can grant to improve intrapreneurs' chances of success—and we'll see how some innovative companies are managing to provide that.

The Case to Include Customers

There are certain advantages to being an intrapreneur rather than an entrepreneur. Working inside a large company, for instance, offers access to operational scale, wide-ranging expertise, and financial as well as physical resources. All these elements are the envy of startups—but if we're talking about the quality of the innovation itself, the one organizational asset that stands high above the rest is an *accessible customer base*. The insights a team can gain by interacting with real potential buyers and beneficiaries of its solution make all the difference to whether that solution will prove valuable.

Ravi Ramaswamy of Philips emphasizes that even though being "customer-led" might sound obvious, it isn't put into practice by many would-be innovators. "I have seen others design products that they *believe* are right for the world," he says, because they "sit in an ivory tower and *think* about what the customer needs." Instead, he advises, "get close to the customer. Ask the customer what they want. Look at how the customer is using your product."

The approach worked like magic when Ramaswamy and his team developed their radically simplified portable ECG machine.

If more and more innovators these days have become believers in what Ramaswamy's preaching, we have the "design thinking" and "lean startup" movements to thank. Both have caught fire in innovation circles as powerful sets of principles and tools for turning early-stage ideas into viable solutions.[1] It's a tenet of both schools of thought (and also of jugaad innovation) that innovators should not assume they know what customers want nor think it's sufficient to hear what people say in focus groups. They have to get out of their offices and track their customers in the wild. Then they need to put a prototype in the customer's hands that shows at least some potential for solving a problem—this is a low-resolution "minimum viable product" versus a fully realized solution—and improve on it through quick, customer-informed iterations. Picasso once said that "an idea is a point of departure and no more. As soon as you elaborate it, it becomes transformed by thought."[2] When the idea is for a new commercial offering, a good portion of that thought should be contributed by the customer.

Involving customers in an innovation early is valuable because their feedback at that point can substantially guide how the solution takes shape, rather than just tweak the final details. Chances are much greater that the novel offering will meet their need. This is how things are done at UnitedHealth Group, for example, whose internal corporate intrapreneurship program bases its process on lean startup principles. Of the five phases in its "enterprise lean" concept, the first three—assessing the problem-market fit, the solution-market fit, and the product-market fit—involve deep interactions with customers.

The first phase is about surfacing customer pain points and figuring out just how much of a pain they really are. These intrapreneurs consider questions like: "Are customers hacking their way to a solution now—where they just have to figure *something* out?" And is the problem "so painful that it's costing them treasure and time?" Discovering big opportunities requires empathic interviewing— getting out and talking to people, and trying to distinguish between a "morphine pain" versus an "aspirin pain." In subsequent phases, similarly nuanced conversations help the team understand how much of a market there is for a solution, and whether the current version of a solution holds great enough appeal.

Even beyond the obvious upside for solution design, intrapreneurs benefit from customer contact. We know that employee engagement rises, for example, when they are able to meet customers and see the impact the enterprise's products and services have on them. This effect is even stronger for the intrapreneurs who are driven to improve those solutions. And when a customer takes an interest in an intrapreneurial project, that can provide another form of air cover (discussed in chapter 4). As Ramaswamy puts it, "Once you start relating to the customer, you find that small delays or mishaps get absolved, because he's been involved in the process."

In a classic *Harvard Business Review* article titled "Managing in the White Space," Mark Maletz and Nitin Nohria shared the story of an intrapreneurial team getting air cover from customers' interest in its work. In this case, the team was inside an industrial components supplier and was trying to launch a lower-end line of products that some powerful colleagues feared would cannibalize the company's high-end sales. When team members talked with anyone about the effort, "they made it clear that they had listened carefully to *customers* and were working to cut through the company's bureaucracy," Maletz and Nohria wrote. "In doing so, they occupied the strategic high ground and made it difficult for others to oppose them."[3]

Customer access also gives intrapreneurial teams a source of legitimizing metrics—that is, objective ways to track and report their progress. Coming up with the right metrics for early stage innovation work is notoriously difficult; everyone seems to get that the yardsticks established for mature lines of business don't apply, but it's hard to come up with similarly rigorous alternatives. Intuit founder Scott Cook is a big believer in what he calls "love metrics"[4]—which might sound soft but can actually be assessed with some precision. How much do people love the idea of the product? Did they recommend it to their peers? How often do they come back? These kinds of measures can be more than sufficient to confirm a team's hypotheses or prove the need for a course correction. In a blog post for Inuit Labs,

Vijay Anand wrote that Cook often coaches their team that if you're not getting high activity from the users you already have, it's time to pivot. That thinking permeates Intuit's managerial ranks. On the subject of how to assess the value of an innovation in progress, Anand continued: "When a team asks me if something is a good idea, I ask them for their unit of one—the one customer their product will delight. And once that works, I tell them to bring me 100. When 100 delighted customers actively use a product, I know there's something to it."[5]

THE SHIFT: LET CUSTOMERS TAKE THE LEAD

From	To
Launching the "perfect" product based on assumptions	Testing small ideas with customers early and often
Keeping the customer at arm's length	Bringing customers into the innovation team via codesign and feedback
Initiatives led by R&D, designers, and developers	Customer-led initiatives

Looking Through a Customer Lens

Many innovators are familiar with the story of the GE Adventure Series—which involves turning dark, scary CT scanning tunnels into inviting storybook hideaways for young patients. I mention it here because it shows how customer access pays off on multiple levels for an intrapreneurial effort.

First, it was by visiting a customer's facility—the pediatric oncology department of a major hospital—that industrial designer Doug Dietz recognized a customer problem crying out for a better solution. He tells the story of how he had just finished working on a CT design project and thought he'd done a wonderful job. He was very proud of himself, and in 2005 he went to one of the hospitals where the equipment was being installed for the first time. But it only took an hour of observation for him to realize how reductively he had pursued his mission. The first people he watched interacting with the new machinery were a family with a young child. The child was so terrified by the machine that she needed to be sedated. He also saw the anxiety of her parents as their frightened child went through the CT procedure. He watched them leave looking distressed and exhausted. Even now, his eyes well up when he recalls the question that occurred to him in that moment: *What was the car ride home like for that family?* That had been his failing as a designer, he realized: thinking only about the device and the procedure and not about how the whole experience would leave the patient and family feeling.[6]

GE Healthcare is in the business of engineering medical devices. Its expertise is in imaging technology, not child psychology. There was very little chance that the idea would dawn on its industrial engineers, sitting back at their workstations, that they needed to reframe the problem in this way. Dietz had to be there to get that the key to better outcomes—including better image capture, higher machine utilization, and better patient experience—was decreasing the need for sedation. It wasn't just about making machines more capable; it was about making children—and families—more comfortable.

Second, it was because of customer collaboration that the GE Adventure Series was as good as it was. There are two layers of customers for a CT machine—the patient who experiences it and the institution that purchases it—and Dietz and his design and engineering colleagues immersed themselves in both groups. On the patient level, they hosted sessions with kids and spent time with visitors to the highly engaging exhibits at the Betty Brinn Children's Museum. On the buyer level, they partnered with radiology departments to create what would work best for them. Listen to Bob Schwartz describe the installation at the University of California San Francisco Benioff Children's Hospital: "We worked collaboratively with them to make a connection to the hospital's environment, integrating things in the Bay area that children and families would recognize—like cable cars, the coastal aspects of where they are, Muir Woods—and to add technology and features we hadn't done before. There was a lot of [informational] material created so that when children see this for the first time . . . they can already be in the story that they're going to find when they get to the hospital."

Third, the fact that there were paying customers who were interested certainly helped the business unit get behind the innovation. Schwartz talked about the huge boost the effort got when it caught the eye of Kathleen Kapsin, radiology director of Children's Hospital of Pittsburgh, part of the University of Pittsburgh Medical Center (UPMC).[7] "Kathleen was all in," he said, "and not only was she willing to collaborate with us on the development of the first one to put in her hospital radiology service, but they were also willing to pay us to do it." With that, the team was able to say a customer had purchased the Adventure Series—and not just any customer, but UPMC, a highly regarded institution and very important customer to GE. "That was instant street cred," Schwartz said, which made it easier for internal colleagues to believe the team must be onto something.

Today the GE Adventure Series is in many more hospitals and has expanded its storytelling repertoire to a dozen or so scenarios. It's a commercial success story, and that starts with its being a patient-level success story. UPMC's follow-up analysis showed that while its Children's Hospital performed 351 sedations for CT scans in 2005, that number dropped to just 45 in the very next year, after its Adventure Series "distraction rooms" came online. By the next year it dropped further, to 9. Put another way, sedations were reduced almost 97 percent. Add up all the ways customers guided the intrapreneurs, and it is clear the team's customer access was the really crucial element in achieving this victory. The GE Adventure Series was something Schwartz characterized as "completely out there, off the edge, should never have succeeded"—and yet it did.[8]

Why We Build Barriers Around the Customer

The problem for intrapreneurs is that in an established enterprise getting face time with customers can be like trying to break into Fort Knox. Just because a company says it wants innovation, and knows that successful innovation depends on customer input, doesn't mean the doors swing open to anyone with an idea to test. And things only get harder when the team asking for access to customers is trying to experiment with something truly novel. Alexander Osterwalder, the management theorist behind the "business model canvas," sees a lot of attempts at disruptive innovation rebuffed by colleagues trying to cordon off customers. He summed it up this way: "The sales team might think the innovation team will mess with their bonus structure or raise customer expectations for a new product. The marketing team might think that testing low-fidelity experimental ideas will mess with the brand. The legal team might think business experiments could create liabilities."[9]

Put yourself in any of those teams' shoes and it is easy to see why they are concerned. The best of the "good" reasons to deny access is that it's possible to damage trusting customer relationships built over years by showing up with subpar ideas and experiments that go nowhere. A team experimenting with new offerings might have the philosophy that even if they fail, valuable lessons will be learned—but traditional keepers of customer relationships may fear that these interactions erode trust and brand reputation. In the work I do with clients, we find that many customers not only enjoy but appreciate being a part of a smart codesign process.

Other reasons for being stingy with customer access are even less justified. They may simply be reflexive habits of an organization that has always had a centralized approach and disciplined methodology around new product development. Carie Davis, an innovation specialist formerly at Coca-Cola, told me about the new way of thinking that confronted people when she engaged the innovation coaches at Startup Weekend to run sessions in Atlanta. These intense events push teams to move quickly from hatching ideas to

BARRIERS TO LETTING CUSTOMERS LEAD

- Involving customers can feel risky—especially in organizations that need to be "perfect" before interacting with end users.
- Politics—giving customer access to developers, for example, rankles managers who traditionally own and silo customer relationships.
- Organizations may want to monitor all aspects of interactions, creating drag on experiments.

getting market feedback on them by building quick-and-dirty versions, taking them out to real people, and trying to sell them. "That would never happen in everyday life at Coca-Cola because everything has to be controlled," Davis said. "If you're putting something in the market, you've got to be sure." One goal of the exercise was to force people to go against their current instincts, and in doing so recognize that those instincts might often be barriers to innovation.[10]

The worst of the "bad" reasons for blocking access to customers is that powerful salespeople own important customer relationships and serve as gatekeepers, deciding which internal initiatives will be put in front of them. They tend to favor already mature offerings for which they can personally make the pitch more knowledgeably. They get compensated more for closing a big-ticket sale versus some exploratory, co-creation arrangement in which more knowledge than money is being exchanged. And they would always rather go back to the customers they already serve than make the new contacts that an innovative offering might appeal to more.

This lack of motivation for salespeople to put innovations in front of clients is something that has been formally researched. The authors behind a 2010 study called "Antecedents of Salespeople's Reluctance to Sell Radically New Products" conclude that such products have "several aspects that can decrease salespeople's interest in them. For instance, familiarizing themselves and their customers with the new product could be unpleasant, undercompensated, and time-consuming for salespeople. Furthermore, establishing relationships with prospective customers may, for example, be incompatible with efforts to deepen relationships with existing customers, or be socially awkward." And thus, a company's resolve to get new offerings into market can be undone by the very people it entrusts with making the sales.[11]

The Gate Crashers—Becoming Customer-Led

Like all things about cultivating intrapreneurship, being customer-led is no black-and-white matter. Customers are a precious asset to a company and cannot be subjected to endless queries about ill-formed ideas or recruited into too many pilots with low prospects for success. But in general, the objective has to be to this: take organizations that are too biased against granting access to customers, and create environments that are more biased toward allowing it. Because, ultimately, customer-led innovation takes hold faster, yields more revenue, generates valuable intelligence, and creates a market for new solutions.

We see this transition happening slowly and unevenly in several sectors and industry situations that have a natural advantage or vested interest in making innovation customer-led.

The Usual Suspects

First, data-driven organizations such as Amazon and Intuit are aggressively customer-driven when it comes to innovation. (Amazon's immense data analytics capabilities, for example, allow it to know what customers want next sometimes before they do.) Intuit, as well, makes it easy for intrapreneurs to get past the challenge of customer access. As discussed, they guide intrapreneurs to choose one customer whom they believe would be best served by the solution. If that single customer uses the solution and recommends it to others, then the idea is validated for further exploration and development.

One example of this was a product idea called ShopOwner, launched by an Intuit employee in Bangalore. He observed that rural-area store clerks were losing track of sales by relying on their memory to quote prices and create handwritten sales slips. Most did not have on-site computers or cash registers with integrated accounting features, but nearly all had smartphones. His simple solution: an app that bundled point-of-sale accounting, simple inventory management, and printed receipts. Based on that plan, he and his team not only created a prototype but also tested it—in less than a week. Their first customer? The café located within Intuit's own Bangalore office.

That café owner loved the prototype, and it was deemed good enough to scale up for further testing and discovery. According to Vijay Anand, a senior vice president at Intuit, this "unit of one" approach enables a great many ideas to be tested quickly and on the cheap. Meanwhile, collecting data using existing customers provides Intuit with insights that can be leveraged beyond the first experiment, which keeps collaboration front-of-mind for intrapreneurs.

Professional Services Firms

Given that the nature of their work has them constantly interacting with clients and conferring on how to solve evolving problems, people in professional services have a clear advantage as customer-led intrapreneurs.

Heidi Gardner of Harvard Law School is an expert in management professional service firms such as management consultancies, accounting firms, and law practices. When Gardner and some of her colleagues studied how "new practice creation" happens, they found that one of the essential ingredients was a "defensible turf." Translated, that means a practice innovation needs to be acknowledged by others to be considered legit and deserve its own dedicated team and leadership. Staking out that new turf within the firm, then, depends in part on validation by external sources, such as powerful clients "to legitimize the new activity."[12]

Innovation Labs

In addition to the coaching and startup resources they provide to employees with promising ideas, innovation labs, garages, and other dedicated incubation infrastructures we see springing up in so many large, traditional enterprises also create clear pathways and mechanisms for reaching out to customers without getting into trouble.

At Pernod Ricard, for instance, the creation of a separate entity, the Breakthrough Innovation Group, has meant that good ideas can be tested with consumers as a matter of course. Under the guidance of managing director Alain Dufossé, the group focuses on new products and reimagined consumer experiences, all in the name of "building the future of *convivialité*" (or, loosely translated, "sharing a spirit of togetherness").[13]

There are plenty of other separate innovation units that companies have created to overcome this barrier to customers. The Boston-based investment giant Fidelity, for example, created its Fidelity Labs to allow for experiments that couldn't otherwise be pursued, given the nature of its work and the highly regulated sector it operates in. Sean Belka, the head of Fidelity Labs, put it to me this way: "Obviously, the business we're in—this is people's life savings or their children's college money. Experimenting in the real world with that in a production environment is not appropriate." But as a design strategist, he is determined to help his colleagues bring a customer lens to their work. "What we did," he explained, "is create Fidelity Labs to create a safe space for experimentation."

As I talked to the Fidelity team behind one recent innovation, FidSafe, I could feel the energy level go up a notch when the topic turned to their customer interactions. FidSafe is a highly secure, cloud-based space that gives users, even if they are not Fidelity customers, a place to organize all the documents, scans, or photos relevant to their finances—from copies of their birth certificates and social security documentation to statements from all the pension funds, 401(k) accounts, and bank accounts they own to photographs of their prized possessions. The team figured out what features and functionality FidSafe needed to offer by—you guessed it—talking to real customers.

Whether in a professional services firm or a distilled beverages producer, the idea here is the same. Intrapreneurial teams need to interact meaningfully with customers, capture what they learn, and translate that into new products and services to complete the circuit. This is far simpler for the types of organizations I just mentioned, as well as for employees in largely customer-facing positions. Typical employees, however, who work deep in the many layers and functions of industrial organizations, need organizational support, including leadership support, to break down the walls that separate them from customers.

DIY Playbook—Let Customers Lead

We've covered a lot of territory in this chapter, but the main takeaway is simple: organizations that allow intrapreneurs to take their cues from customers create an instant advantage and avoid many of the barriers that derail internal innovation. These are the plays that I have seen work best in industries and environments across the board:

1. Create Leading-Edge Customer Focus
2. Hack Better Access to Customers
3. Turn Customers into Innovation Partners
4. Make Intrapreneurship a Sales Priority

1. Create Leading-Edge Customer Focus

Go lean. The lean startup approach to innovation is worth learning. The whole system is centered on hypothesis-driven experimentation with a focus on regularly speaking to and observing customers as well as taking an analytical approach to the market by acting quickly to build, measure, and learn—fast.

At Deutsche Telekom, a special program for intrapreneurs called UQBATE is based on the lean startup approach; its process is focused on connecting intrapreneurs with customers. Any company with an intrapreneurial support function based on these fundamental lean startup principles needs to create a space in which idea owners have license to and, in fact, *must* involve customers in their iterative development process.

Use design methodology. Like the lean startup approach, design thinking and jugaad innovation are all about seeing things through the eyes of the customer. Intuit was an early convert to design thinking and created a team of "innovation catalysts" to help their intrapreneurs prototype a solution, field an experiment, and interact with customers. That was over a decade ago, and by now the design thinking philosophy has completely taken hold in the organization as a way to keep intrapreneurs connected to customers.

2. Hack Better Access to Customers

Use a "pull" approach. One intrapreneur I know became frustrated spending all his effort trying to persuade colleagues to put a new solution in front of some of the firm's sophisticated clients. Finally he changed tactics and started publishing articles and giving speeches in places where these customers typically encountered new ideas. Sure enough, the clients came to him wanting to know more. When the calls came in from customers, his colleagues were suddenly more willing to arrange meetings. This "pull" approach (rather than "push") enabled him to take control and be more proactive in reaching out to clients.

Piggyback on corporate events. Setting up in public settings to meet customers is a frugal way for intrapreneurs to interact with their target market and access the intelligence they need. For example, when Balanda Atis and her team at L'Oréal were developing foundation for women of color, they needed to be creative to collect the consumer data they needed. Their strategy? Tag along on dozens of regularly scheduled road shows at malls and state fairs. Atis and her team brought their samples and measuring tools and were able to collect skin tone measurements and ask questions directly to the women they wanted to serve. It provided an instant customer connection that was fundamental to their success.

Locate internal customers. If you're working in a consumer goods company with a large enough workforce, you can find real customers among your employees. A senior marketing manager reminded me that it's hard to know "what has legs . . . or what needs to be pivoted or modified" until you've done the experimentation—but even a big company can run only so many tests with customers. "Leveraging employees is a way to do a little early market experimentation without tapping your finite resource pool" of customers.

3. Turn Customers into Innovation Partners

Co-create with customers. The term *co-creation* has been floating around for at least two decades. Coined by C. K. Prahalad and Venkat Ramaswamy, co-creation is "the joint creation of value by the company and the customer; allowing the customer to co-construct the service experience to suit their context."[14] At the global logistics company DHL, a key component of the company's quest for growth is its Customer Innovation Workshops, in which future-thinking DHL team members and important customers "are jointly engaged in developing ideas for new products, services, or processes." One recent high-profile result of this was the Parcelcopter—a realization of the much-anticipated package-delivery drone. In a three-month proof-of-concept project, DHL customers tested the system with some 130 packages delivered to two remote villages in the Bavarian Alps.

Engage each level of customer. Intrapreneurs should consider each successive layer of customer and determine how to include varying perspectives in the design process. We saw how Doug Dietz of GE Healthcare spearheaded the creation of the Adventure Series CT scans after recognizing that while the equipment worked great from the perspective of the manufacturer, it was far less of a success in terms of how young patients reacted to the unfriendly machinery.

Recognize customer accomplishments. Honoring customers that contribute to intrapreneurship deepens the relationship and starts to make a market for new solutions. For instance, the DHL Innovation Center presents an annual award for customers who work with their intrapreneurs. In 2016, the winner of DHL's Most Innovative Customer Solution award was Daimler/Smart, who partnered with DHL Parcel to develop a service that "enables Smart car owners to have their parcels delivered to the trunk of their vehicle."[15] The award is the highlight of the company's annual conference that brings together several hundred logistics professionals, including DHL customers, prospective customers, and supply chain partners.

4. Make Intrapreneurship a Sales Priority

Take intrapreneurship to the front line. A main tenet of the Disrupt-It-Yourself ethos is that intrapreneurship should not be isolated to professional innovators, scientists, and product development teams. Salespeople and others at the front line (at call centers, for example) come up with some of the best ideas of all because they have a direct link to the market and know customers' needs and concerns. You can bet they will be more likely to tap into their customer relationship to validate solutions when they feel the passion.

Incentivize sales to partner with intrapreneurs. We can learn from a number of effective efforts by companies (including Colgate and Citigroup) to set targets for their sales organizations to raise the percentage of revenues that should come from new and innovative products. The manufacturing company 3M came up with this metric decades ago, when it specified that 25 percent of revenues must come from products launched in the past three years. In addition to boosting the profile of innovation, this play gives account managers a clear reason to introduce innovation teams to their customers and do more to help the customer-led innovation pan out.

Executive Scorecard

- Are customers hacking their own solutions to problems in your space? How have you responded?
- Is there an established path for intrapreneurs in your organization to connect with customers and include them in the development of new products and services?
- Are marketing and sales employees motivated and incentivized to support intrapreneurship? Are they a part of the intrapreneurship effort?
- Do the rules and systems that govern your enterprise function to connect intrapreneurs with customers or keep them apart?
- Are customers invited into your innovation process?

SIX

Principle 4: Keep It Fluid

I was impressed to hear how one intrapreneur at a major retail chain managed to put together the multitalented team she needed to make her vision a reality. Her passionately held vision was that the company should make space on its website for the kinds of unique and quirky items made only by smaller manufacturers and artists. As she looked across the current merchandise selection, she worried that the sameness that came with big-box buying was boring—and that customers would gravitate to sellers where they could find more distinctive options. But executing the change she had in mind would be a tall order. In its business-as-usual mode, the retailer's vast size, with its network of stores and tightly managed inventory, meant that it dealt only with large-scale, highly vetted suppliers.

Without a background in procurement, she did not have the experience or contacts to source the items she had in mind.

When she eventually got the idea approved by management for exploration, she was given permission to hire the expertise needed from outside. As she tells the story, she was interviewing consultants and was close to putting a veteran Amazon manager under contract. That's when one of the consultants changed her mind. "Honestly, we could do the work for you," a logistics specialist said, "but you have an insanely good sourcing infrastructure setup [at your own company]. Why wouldn't you just exploit that?"

Good question. The answer, unfortunately, was that the organization was rigidly structured into silos and pyramids, and their processes made it nearly impossible to gain access to expertise in other parts of the business. Anyone with a sufficient budget is inclined to take the path of least resistance and hire from the outside. But in this case, the argument for internal talent was so solid, and her vision of the idea so strong, that it merited an attempt.

To her surprise, once she deftly made it past the management layer (which tends to systematically fend off requests for colleagues' time) and connected with the supply chain staff she needed, she found them eager to join her. She learned that some of them already shared her concern: the company was missing out on a vibrant artisanal movement it had the capabilities to tap into. None had acted on the idea because it seemed like such a radical change to instigate from where they sat in the organization.

Now, sensing an opening, her colleagues jumped at the chance to take part in something potentially transformational. Even in the early days of the project, when she could tap only 20 percent of their time, progress was so rapid it surprised even the team itself. It was a win-win: she benefited from world-class expertise without spending extra money to hire external consultants, and her colleagues were energized and engaged by the creative demands of a project they believed in. It was just one project, but it helped send a message more broadly: the experts the company had throughout its ranks should not be so tightly bound to their routine job descriptions that they couldn't support its innovation goals. The approach to DIY initiatives could and should be much more fluid.

THE SHIFT: KEEP IT FLUID

From	To
Complicated organizational structure	Clean line from innovation front lines to C-suite
Hierarchy and silos	Self-organizing project teams
Centralized and insular innovation	Building relationships throughout the organization

In Search of Fluidity

This story points to another big principle of Disrupt-It-Yourself: *keep it fluid*. Intrapreneurs inside DIY organizations need to be able to identify and connect with specialists across the organization with minimal friction. They need to unite with people who have shared interests and relevant skills to form ad hoc project teams. And since this fluid team formation does not happen naturally in most organizations, companies need light structures to enable new levels of information sharing, networking, and mobility across their talent pools.

We've known for decades that to compete in increasingly competitive and dynamic markets, enterprises must become nimbler. Steady, incremental progress along a course set in the past is not an option in markets where more agile competitors constantly innovate and change. It has also become clear that to respond nimbly to emerging opportunities, organizations must be able to pull teams together spontaneously with the right combinations of strengths. *Adhocracy* is the term that Warren Bennis coined years ago for an organization that operates in this mode, in clear contrast to the usual bureaucracy. It's an appealing vision, that individuals with vital and complementary talents could emerge, *Avengers*-style, from the far corners of an enterprise at a moment's notice and hit the ground running as a productive team.

This is not what happens naturally in the traditional organizational structure used to achieve scale in slower, more stable environments. That traditional structure has been a pyramid or at best a matrix, with clear lines of command running through many layers of well-defined jobs, all easily labeled in a classic org chart. Across millennia, that was the only structure that could handle the coordinated information flows required to keep a vast army of people moving toward the same overall objective. Today things are dramatically different. Communications and information technologies make other coordination mechanisms possible, and decades-old bureaucratic models must be updated in order to stay relevant.

Take the "Holacracy" concept that Tony Hsieh, founder of the online shoe retailer Zappos, has advocated.[1] Its philosophy is that two major rationales for the old way of structuring and governing organizations are now irrelevant. First, because communication is cheap and easy, you don't need a top-down control structure to ensure that everyone understands and is working toward the same goal. Second, because things change much faster and less predictably in today's competitive markets, it makes no sense to optimize an organization for unquestioning execution of strategies set by "leaders" long ago and far away. Holacracy wants to achieve control by distributing power, not centralizing it. Hsieh likes to draw a contrast between thriving cities and traditional companies: when a city doubles in size, research shows that its productivity per resident typically rises by 15 percent, but as companies expand, their productivity drifts downward. "So we're trying to figure out how to structure Zappos more like a city," he says, "and less like a bureaucratic corporation." The key to the difference is that cities are self-organizing systems—all the actors within them just do what they individually think is right, without being told what must be done by, say, the mayor. In a company that has adopted Holacracy, employees "act more like entrepreneurs and self-direct their work instead of reporting to a manager who tells them what to do."[2]

In a lot of ways, Holacracy is an outgrowth of an earlier line of thinking that had many management theorists pointing to the "Hollywood model" of serving a demanding market hungry for hit after hit. In any major filmmaking center, people with visions for projects they want to pursue have access to an entire ecosystem of funders, firms, and freelancers, from which they assemble all the capabilities they need and can afford. Consultants to other kinds of businesses have advised their clients to migrate closer to filmmaking's project-centered model. This would mean figuring out how to create that kind of richly capable ecosystem inside a firm, as well as making the boundaries of the firm very porous, so that people running projects could have maximum flexibility to involve the external contributors and partners they needed.

Going back even further to 1990, an executive named Lars Kolind arrived at the Danish company Oticon with a bold new structural idea he called "the spaghetti organization." If you think about the clean boxes and lines on the traditional command-and-control organization chart, and then you think about what happens to those lines in a Holacratic or Hollywood system, you see where he got his metaphor. To the great surprise of the engineers working on Oticon's innovative hearing aids, as well as all its functional groups from finance to sales and from HR to PR, Kolind in one fell swoop did away with everyone's job title and moved them all from their accustomed offices and desks too. Most important, he told them that it was up to them now to decide where their talents could be best applied. No one would be assigned to projects where they would receive top-down mandates from project bosses. Instead, projects would be posted on a central bulletin board, and employees could gravitate to the ones they saw as the best fit for their skills or as an opportunity to develop new skills that would make them more capable. Once they were on a team, they were expected to be as much in charge of it as anyone else. Project "leaders" were only there to provide the necessary coordination and support, not to be the delegators and decision makers telling the rest what to do. The organizing principle was the goal of the project itself, and the whole team equally shared the responsibility of figuring out how to achieve it and fairly distributing the necessary work among themselves.

Ultimately, Oticon's radical experiment gave way to a more conventional restructuring as a matrix organization. Why? Some management hadn't fully committed to the model (the company didn't give up hierarchy altogether—and the perks of what was left of traditional business may have been too good to encourage lasting change), and in the model itself, employees may have been overly focused on only the most high-profile projects or overextending themselves. But remarkably, "spaghetti" served the company very well for almost a decade. It worked as long as it did, most agree, because the company's sense of purpose, as a hearing-aid producer, was so focused. Everyone in the company had a very clear idea about the customer and the job to be done for that customer, and they shared an excitement about the breakthroughs that could be made with advancing technology, without being territorial about who did what. Innovation was something everyone was on board with and wanted to be part of in the most effective way possible—not in a predefined way.

Should your company try something similarly radical? When Kolind sent his first memo explaining the new approach to his whole workforce, the title on it was "Think the Unthinkable"— and "unthinkable" still describes how this level of organizational disruption would be received by most companies. But short of complete transformation, there are many things managers can do to create more flexibility in how projects are initiated and staffed. The question top management should be asking itself is: If the goal is "keeping it fluid" with respect to how teams form and disband, how do we provide the platforms and communication tools to enable that? How do we encourage it to happen, reward it when it does, and generally change the norms that guide our people's daily behavior?

Companies must shift toward a more fluid model, even if they cannot give up their bureaucratic org charts and processes altogether. But to succeed with more fluidity, they will need new mechanisms for (1) coordinating and aligning the efforts of self-managing teams, (2) for encouraging symbiotic behavior among people who no longer have clear and consistent reporting lines and group identity, (3) for motivating and recognizing great work in the absence of clear paths for promotion, and (4) for identifying those people who should be given more responsibility and bigger roles in ensuring the company's future success.

Create a Team of Teams

General Stanley McChrystal would recognize what Tony Hsieh did at Zappos or Lars Kolind did at Oticon as variations on a "team of teams" approach, his phrase for an entire organization made up of agile, independent teams that nevertheless manage to align and achieve shared goals. This is the model he credits with turning the tide in the US military's fight against al-Qaeda in Iraq after he took control of the Joint Special Operations Command (JSOC) in 2003. McChrystal reconceived JSOC as a team of teams because he wanted the advantages of small groups—such as direct communications, fast decision-making, and agility to respond to evolving conditions—while operating on the scale required to accomplish very big objectives. At UnitedHealth Group, managers throughout the organization read McChrystal's best-selling book on his team of teams approach[3] and translated it to their own vast workforce. Deb Sundal, who drives innovation projects as a senior vice president there (in the Enterprise R&D function's product architecture group) told me she and her colleagues like the model because it starts with an assumption that responsibility for innovation will not be centralized but can "live close to the problems" in highly distributed "communities of innovation" across the enterprise.

That also sounds like a good description of what ING Group did when it flattened the organization chart for its twenty thousand employees over a two-year period and created highly empowered teams it calls "squads." According to the company's chief information officer, Peter Jacobs, the transformation was inspired by the realization that even though ING is a financial services company, it is really an information technology company and thus should take its cues from other tech innovators, such as Facebook, Google, Netflix, Spotify, and Uber. "The interesting thing," he told *McKinsey Quarterly*, "is that none of these companies operate in the same industry or share a common purpose. One is a media company, another is search-engine based, and another one is in the transport business. What they all have in common is a particular way of working and a distinctive people culture. In most cases they work in small fluid teams that are united in a common purpose, follow an agile 'manifesto,' interact closely with customers, and are constantly able to reshape what they are working on."[4]

BARRIERS TO KEEPING IT FLUID

- Involves structural change, which challenges hierarchy
- Shifts the decision-making role of managers, HR, legal, and others
- Means teaming must be a core capability
- Requires full senior management and board support

The squads at ING are each led by an owner responsible for a product or service. There are "chapter leaders," who are subject-matter experts, and "customer journey experts," who keep their focus on customer relationships. The old walls between marketing specialists, product and commercial specialists, user-experience designers, data analysts, and IT engineers have been torn down. Now all of these sit together in multidisciplinary teams dedicated to solving client needs and aligned by a common vision of what ING's brand should stand for. Bart Schlatmann, former chief operational officer of ING, summed up the transformation in an interview: "We gave up traditional hierarchy, formal meetings, overengineering, detailed planning, and excessive 'input steering' in exchange for empowered teams, informal networks, and 'output steering.'"[5]

Small work group empowerment has also been a major theme at China's Haier Group under the leadership of Ruimin. Zhang was convinced that to compete in markets that increasingly reward innovation, his company's organizational structure would have to do more to unlock the potential of its people. He also wanted to do away with the bureaucratic gridlock of the typical huge enterprise. He saw a more powerful model in a system of networked teams. To transform an efficiency-oriented monolith, he decided to radically redesign the structure in which some fifty thousand employees worldwide do their daily work, with an eye to increasing its agility. Smaller units, he decided, could move faster. What was before a classic pyramid was transformed into a distributed network of more than four thousand self-managed, cross-functional units, each including members with skills in research and development, supply chain management, and sales and marketing. Because these units share the same basic structure and processes, they are able to operate in a loosely coupled way.[6]

Haier's small intrapreneurial cells today hold the power to interact directly with customers and to make decisions autonomously based on what they learn. To make this bottom-up, customer-centric organizational structure work, Zhang transformed the idea of a manager from being commander and supervisor to supporter and provider, responsible for connecting self-managing units with the resources they need to serve customer needs as responsively as possible. To him, it does not make sense to give managers greater decision-making power than this because "they are not directly in touch with customers."

Each unit therefore operates as a unique profit center and must hold its own in a larger organization full of other capable and focused teams. But each also has the benefit of being part of a massive multinational corporation, with access to rich resources and high-level air cover. Haier's organizational agility enables it to react swiftly to rapidly changing—or unexpected—customer needs and innovate faster, better, and cheaper than its rivals. For instance, in China, any call placed to its national customer service center is answered within three rings and a technician is dispatched to the customer's house within three hours—even on Sundays. Some years ago, one such call came from a farmer in a remote village in Sichuan province who complained about the constantly clogged drainpipe in his washing machine. The Haier technician who went to investigate found that the farmer was using the machine daily to wash the dirt off his freshly harvested potatoes. The mud was causing the clogging. "Most companies would react by saying, 'This machine is not designed for this purpose,'" noted Philip Carmichael, Haier's president for the Asia-Pacific region, "but Haier's approach was to say, 'This guy [the farmer] probably isn't the only one who's tried to wash potatoes. Is there a way to adapt this product to this requirement? Maybe we can make a machine that actually washes potatoes and clothes.'"[7]

Haier's flexible thinking was spot-on: it turns out that many farmers across China needed a better solution for washing their produce. Sensing a market opportunity, Haier's cross-functional teams quickly acted on their intuition by developing a washing machine with larger pipes that could handle the silt. The product was a hit among farmers. But Haier's creative teams didn't stop there. They also invented a washing machine that can peel potatoes and even designed an appliance for herders in Inner Mongolia and the Tibetan Plateau to help churn yak milk into butter. These atypical inventions, built on mental and organizational agility, eventually inspired Haier to introduce in 2009 a washing machine able to wash clothes without detergent. That groundbreaking innovation helped propel Haier to the number-one position in the laundry equipment market not only in China but around the world.

More generally, as an organization capable of adapting fluidly and quickly to unforeseen threats and opportunities, Haier continues to grow. Its networked, team-based structure is well suited to its complex market environment. In Zhang's own favorite phrase, he has succeeded in "making a big company small" and giving a very large business the flexibility of an agile startup.

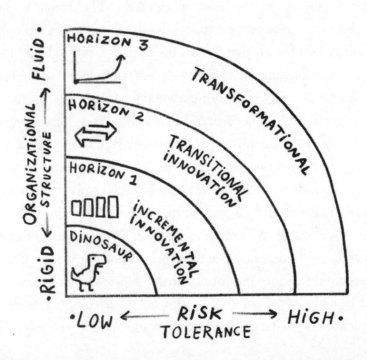

Keep People Fluid

In chapter 1, I mentioned Marc Nager's description of the ideal intrapreneurial team. The phrase he used has been popular ever since Rei Inamoto, a former chief creative officer at an ad agency, used it at a SXSW conference in 2012. "To run an efficient team, you only need three people: a hipster, a hacker, and a hustler," Inamoto said. "When I look at the better teams I've been a part of, this has absolutely proven to be true."[8] Hipsters, he went on to explain, often come up with the cool new ideas, and throughout projects they keep asserting their sense of what will appeal to leading-edge customers. Hackers are the ones with the technical chops to make quick progress on prototypes and understand what is feasible at scale. Hustlers are the extroverts who can get in front of funders and buyers and make the sale. In the entrepreneurial world, the expectation is not that these three people will find each other and marry for life. Rather, a "3H" team coalesces around an opportunity and then just as easily disbands when that project comes to a close.

Some types of enterprises find it easier to keep it fluid in this way because they have the natural advantage of doing work that lends itself to discrete projects rather than constant, steady flows of routine work. Take USAID, for example (more formally, the United States Agency for International Development). This federal agency serves US national security and foreign policy goals by promoting the economic stability and growth required for enduring peace in many parts of the world. With teams spread around the globe, all seeking better approaches to public health, emergency humanitarian assistance, and more, USAID decided in 2014 to create a hub to collect, test, and share innovation. The mission of this hub, called the Global Development Lab, is to "deliver new innovations, tools, and approaches for accelerating development impact and to transform the way we do development work."

As part of the US federal government, USAID has its share of bureaucracy, but it also knows that fluidity is central to its operations. The people I met at USAID are part of the Global Development Lab, supporting the efforts of people doing innovative work on projects out in the field. Chief of Innovative Design Seema Patel doesn't hesitate to reach out and collaborate with pretty much anyone across the enterprise. "It's a fluid organization," she said. "I don't feel like I need anyone's permission to exchange ideas or even plan projects together. That way of working creates a freedom that you don't see within a lot of corporate environments that are structured into management strata."

In companies that encourage greater fluidity, valuable connections can be made in all kinds of ways. Recall Babak Forutanpour's brown-bag lunch groups at Qualcomm. The point was to mix people together who would not ordinarily interact, and to get them bouncing ideas off each other. Over a five-year period, his original group of eight coconspirators grew into an intrapreneurial movement of three thousand employees working on hundreds of inventive ideas and hacker-style solutions on the side. The great thing about these teams is that they were self-organizing and autonomous—no one issued orders—and they all operated in a similar way. With Forutanpour's simple model and a shared excitement for innovation, people were able to create a huge amount of new value for the company. Likewise for Ravi Ramaswamy's innovators in Bangalore: "Today, when I sit back and look," he told me, "I see another fifty or sixty people like me working on what we can do in other markets." As a result, "the number of products that we have in the market has gone up exponentially."

Where fluidity really pays off is in settings where units have enough flexibility to release people from their normal day-to-day duties when an opportunity arises that calls for their talent. At Amazon, for example, the expectation is that employees will be the source of most new business ideas. And thousands of them submit proposals for innovations of all kinds through the working backwards process mentioned in chapter 4. In a recent *Forbes* article about the process, Amazon's consumer business chief, Jeff Wilke, told the story of a young woman whose proposal had just been approved for further development. But before she heard the news, she had moved into a new position in the company. She was taken aback when Wilke not only gave the project the green light but asked if she wanted to run the new business.[9] A day later, she accepted. The fact that such an impromptu reassignment was even possible says as much about the boss who had just promoted her as about the woman herself. At Amazon, that kind of fluidity in response to an opportunity is not seen as a nuisance but as central to how the organization works.

Whether it's a team as small as three people or a larger one, it stands to reason that the composition of structures, skills, and personalities that is right for one innovation initiative won't be identical to another. Sorting out just the right teams to go after a range of interesting opportunities will be a continuous and never-ending process. It is also bound to sometimes be downright messy. Yet, for companies that rise to the challenge, the payoff can be immense in terms of ongoing innovation and, yes, creating a Disrupt-It-Yourself organization.

DIY Playbook—Keep It Fluid

Fluidity delivers more control and autonomy to individual intrapreneurs and small groups, and less to the management layers above them. This tricky little paradigm switch packs a positive punch that promises to increase innovation if managed properly. The trouble is that the type of organizational structure that enables fluidity is less rigid than we are accustomed to today. Just as everything digital tears down existing walls, we need to eliminate artificial, outdated boundaries and allow intrapreneurs some latitude to self-direct, self-manage, and self-organize. Here's a look at how to make it work:

1. Create a Team of Teams
2. Make Management Fluid
3. Support Agility Through Structure

1. Create a Team of Teams

Support fluid teams. Organizations must institutionalize how they support teams. Again: support, don't control; eliminate rigid, outdated bureaucracy; give teams resources to achieve their goals; and create a culture that accepts responsibility and expects some measure of failure. Do whatever it takes to empower teams to succeed.

Allow room to self-organize. Intrapreneurial activity thrives in organizations that are not overly rigid about roles or too sectioned into silos to allow some creative self-organization. If you want to see new ideas bubbling up and turning into valuable new offerings and ways of working, you must enable teams to form and disband on their own based on your people's shared passions and varying skills. You must find ways to set hierarchy aside and ensure the free flow of information that allows colleagues to become aware of each other's initiatives. Whether or not you go as far as Tony Hsieh using the model of Holacracy at Zappos, think of what he is trying to achieve with it and how you might move closer to that as well.

Keep fluidity simple. You may have heard of Amazon's "two pizza rule." When Jeff Bezos recognized that teams needed to be less constrained and more efficient, he mandated small, highly autonomous groups—with no more members than could be fed with two pizzas. His simple solution swept away a barrier to fluidity.

Get agile. The agile software development methodology is an obvious place to look to inspire action and identify a path for organizational fluidity. It presents a set of principles under which requirements and solutions evolve through the collaborative effort of self-organizing cross-functional teams. Begin by reading the "Agile Manifesto," published in 2001 by a set of forward-thinking software developers.[10] Cherry-pick the parts of the agile way you can use to evolve your organization. Agile principles are closely linked to the fast and frugal approach of *Jugaad Innovation*, and Eric Reis centered his foundational book, *The Lean Startup*, around it.

2. Make Management Fluid

Rethink the role of managers. Fluidity is made more manageable in organizations with far fewer management layers. Yet the role of managers should morph, not disappear. The job of line managers at ING, for example, is to coach and mentor teams, remain informed, act as advisers, and gain trust and followership—not to focus on adherence to process.

Measure for fluidity. More and more, we celebrate leaders who collaborate, make connections, and empower their teams to set goals and make their own decisions within the context of an overarching strategy or business plan. This in turn requires organizations to rethink the traditional orientation of goal and performance management within the context of teams.

Prepare to get messy. Fluidity drives intrapreneurship, but it is seldom neat and clean. Managers need to adapt their structure, empower people to experiment, and learn from what does *not* work in order to leverage everything that does.

3. Support Agility Through Structure

Make tech fluid. Software tools for goal sharing, information sharing, and project sharing are all part of creating fluidity. Consider technologies like Slack, Hive, Pivotal Tracker, and others. Then standardize and implement them as a component of the organization's IT and HR management system. Or don't, if it's simply too hard for your organization to integrate at scale—but make sure it's easy for your intrapreneurs to use these on the side without a lot of red tape.

Get centered. Centralized or separate innovation centers can help design the standard for fluidity as well as help you set up structures to put self-organizing teams in place within an organization.

Executive Scorecard

- Does your organizational structure support intrapreneurship by allowing people to move fluidly across the organization to collaborate for innovation and problem-solving?

- What place do empowered teams play in your organizational culture?
- Do your management and performance measurement systems support fluidity and agility?
- Have you found ways to allow the "messiness" that fosters intrapreneurship and innovation?

SEVEN

Principle 5: Maximize Return on Intelligence

In 2016 and 2017, I worked with Stanley Black & Decker's Global Emerging Markets group to help them explore ways to accelerate their growth in rapidly developing economies such as India, China, and Brazil. It was a major aspiration—so why think small? The plan was to bypass incremental product improvements and leap right into business model innovation as a way to meet the needs of emerging market customers, with a focus on the tradespeople who work as carpenters, plumbers, and electricians. We started with a disciplined ethnographic study of the markets to create a foundation of knowledge. The lessons learned from this "walk in their shoes" research formed the basis of several compelling hypotheses that we eventually formed into eight potentially viable business model opportunities.

The next phase? Fast and frugal experimentation.

We prioritized each of the business models and acted rapidly to experiment with our top picks in the marketplace—without breaking the bank. In India, for instance, our research highlighted a critical need to "meet users where they are," both physically and by targeting their unique needs. The insight culminated in new business model design including mobile services for tool distribution and tool repair. We began the focused experiment with just a couple of vans and a handful of motorcycles serving locations that were popular with local tradespeople.

To extract the most knowledge out of these experiments, we tracked thirteen input and outcome metrics over a four-week period, including average repair time, miles driven, total tool repair sales, and van-related direct costs. The result? Copious amounts of data about customers collected at very low cost that were quickly integrated back into a more refined business model design of this new way to reach and serve customers.

Sam Reid, cofounder of Ideas2Impact and one of our partners in the effort, made the point that the initiative was as much about what we could learn for calibrating future ventures as it was about success in any one experiment. "A lot of organizations spend time telling people to celebrate failure, 'fail fast,' 'fail forward,' etc., in the hopes that their teams will overcome a lifetime of seeing failure as bad because their boss, teachers, and others say they should," he said. "This may work for some, but we've found it more useful to just call the outcome of whatever we do 'learning.' When we do well, it's learning. When we don't, it's learning. By focusing everyone on capturing and applying new insights from innovation efforts, we've turned the whole process into more of a continuous journey towards becoming smarter, faster, and better versus a win/lose event."

Reid is right. Each of our experiments and their metrics allowed us to quickly and inexpensively test models that otherwise would have been rolled out in large-scale pilots. Our series of small experiments enabled multiple iterations and adjustments at low to no cost—saving money by allowing insights to arrive earlier, before a massive rollout was required.

The takeaway is that intrapreneurs can deliver value via insight and learning long before they are celebrated as successful innovators. Every idea tested with customers helps fine-tune a solution—or indicate what not to do next time. Every new attempt at change delivers data about how to become better. In addition, looking at learning as a kind of currency creates a corporate culture that is more risk tolerant. And when these insights are shared across the organization (rather than swept under the carpet), others can benefit from this learning—helping build a corporate culture willing to test ideas and take smart risks.

Stanley Black & Decker knows a bit about aspiring to create a culture of experimentation. Jaime Ramirez, who is president for global emerging markets at the company, said, "We are committed to being a learning organization, and we don't want to put up barriers to innovation by settling for business-as-usual approaches. This is an ongoing process and we need to remain open-minded to fully benefit from it."

The New World ROI—Return on Intelligence

Not every project needs to succeed in traditional ROI (return on investment) terms, but the work should leave everyone smarter for having done it. Sean Belka of Fidelity Labs, for instance, told me this: "Our goal is not to push something through every time.

It is to utilize our methodology to execute on a robust learning agenda—the outcome of which may be to stop and redeploy these resources." Similarly, Cristina Notermann at Target said her favorite intrapreneurial team motto is "Follow the learnings"— and explained that it can lead to several distinct behaviors, only one of which would be to execute the plan.

Another way I've heard this put is: "Risk equals 'unknowns' times investment." What this means is that one way to dial down the risk associated with a new venture is to invest less money in it. And an alternative way is to gain more information and therefore trim the unknowns that make success uncertain. Typically, the result of information gathering is some kind of course correction by the team—and the sooner the better. A manager at a large candy manufacturer told me, "We don't want to spend too much time chasing down a path" that ultimately won't work, he said. "We want to learn quickly and adjust, so that a bad idea gets canceled or gets pivoted to a better idea."

My term for what they are all orbiting around is "return on *intelligence*"—a reformulation of ROI that puts the short-term emphasis on intellectual rather than financial gains. Of course, intelligence gains ultimately translate into performance gains for an enterprise, and using my kind of ROI leads to more appropriate metrics for new ventures.

This philosophy resonates with entrepreneurs in high-potential startups, whose strategy is to get something simple out fast so they can learn from it and start improving upon it. The big question, as Salim Ismail told me, is: "What's the smallest feature footprint that allows you to get to market and get feedback from users?" He likes to point out that the initial public versions of Twitter, Foursquare, and Facebook were "quite flaky" with their flawed design and questionable user interaction. "But they iterated rapidly with initial customer data and were ultimately successful." Why? Because they learned—and applied those learnings.

It was the same with Reddit, which now ranks as the fourth-most-visited website in the United States and eighth in the world. Alexis Ohanian, who cofounded the site with Steve Huffman, said that at the outset, they were "just two dudes in a room . . . [who] had no idea what we were doing—no idea at all." But they learned fast, with an attitude of "that's what life is, just figuring stuff out." His advice to other innovators is to accept that "the first version of everything is janky" but "don't let that stop you from putting stuff out in the world."[1]

Intrapreneurial projects pay return on intelligence by leaving the people who come later older and wiser as business builders. One manager working in an incubator unit of a large company told me about the "depository he started—almost an internal Google of ideas." Say an intrapreneur comes up with a great idea about x, he explained. "Okay, type in x—and out comes fifteen x-related ideas that people have worked on in the last two years." The depository will provide immediate access to documents and status information, and also the contact information of the team to connect and determine: "What can I learn from them? What worked and did not work for them?"

Whether a digital repository, a simple app, or even just the company blog, organizations need a mechanism for capturing learnings from experimental forays. The idea is to save other teams from reinventing the wheel or reinvestigating paths that you already know lead down a blind alley. By institutionalizing intelligence, innovators allow future teams to make progress faster, yielding undeniable value. Another name for this is "reinvested learnings."

THE SHIFT: MAXIMIZE RETURN ON INTELLIGENCE

From	To
Traditional metrics	New KPIs that support intrapreneurship and disruption
Rewarding only results in the current scenario	Rewarding insights for the unknown and the future
Traditional corporate culture	A culture that does not fear disruption
Intrapreneurship as a fun idea	Intrapreneurship as a core competency and disciplined approach

Measure to Leverage Learning

The trick is to capture insight and record learnings before they seep back into the floorboards of the garage, lab, or office park where they were produced. That's where metrics come into play.

Wait—did I hear a collective groan? Mention "performance metrics" and people on all sides of an innovation effort shrink back. Or on a more positive note, they may tell you about those happy occasions when they escaped measurement.

Bob Schwartz at GE, for example, recalled when the CEO of his division told another colleague: "I can measure sales, and I can measure variable cost productivity, and I can measure manufacturing speed and shipping times—but that stuff that Schwartz and his team does, I can't measure it. I can't figure out how to put a metric around it. All I know is that every time they do it, I sell more stuff."

Selling more stuff is something that organizations can get behind. But metrics? Intrapreneurs worry they will lead to projects being weeded out before they have the chance to grow. This is often why innovation teams demand a degree of separation from the main business. As much as most of us in big business might nod that, yes, new initiatives must be measured differently, we can't help reverting to our accustomed yardsticks—and periodically using them to rap the knuckles of innovators.

BARRIERS TO MAXIMIZING RETURN ON INTELLIGENCE

- Difficult for organizations that don't put a high value on learning
- Requires new metrics, KPIs, and other accountability measures
- Its value is nonfinancial at first
- Organizations with a heavy focus on traditional ROI struggle to make the shift

Performance metrics—*you can't live with 'em and you can't kill 'em*. Innovators need metrics to keep them on track, and organizations need them to measure progress. And in the case of innovation, they both need them to ensure that intrapreneurial behavior takes hold and spreads out across the enterprise.

Making Metrics Manageable

Without transparency around goals and clarity about how a project is progressing, we would never know how to measure success. But where do we begin measuring? Jeff Zias at Intuit believes that the right metrics for innovation need to be examined and debated on at least three levels:

1. the top level of overall innovation performance by the firm;
2. the midlevel of the performance of its innovation program

(that is, whatever formal structure and processes it has put in place, perhaps under the direction of a chief innovation officer); and

3. the initiative level for individual teams to track and report their progress.

That top level is what the company-level innovation rankings produced by *Fortune* and *Forbes* try to gauge with their algorithms based on publicly available data.[2] For Intuit, Zias said, the overall goal is simply stated but hard to measure. "I believe the right innovation metrics have to do with 'Are we actually improving our customers' lives in a way that they most care about over time?' So it's this notion of measuring the actual improvement across *everything* we should be focused on, knowing 'What do the customers find valuable, and are we continuously improving that?'"

A level down from there, if an innovation function has been established—maybe in the form of a lab, hub, garage, or center—top management needs metrics to know how it is doing. At this level, managers puzzle over what to measure. When the newsletter *Innovation Leader* surveyed 198 senior innovation executives in 2014 about what kinds of measures they were using, it discovered quite a mix of "activity" and "impact" metrics.

The five most commonly used metrics were: (1) revenue generated by new products; (2) number of projects in the innovation pipeline; (3) stage-gate-specific metrics—that is, projects moving from one stage to the next; (4) P&L impact or other financial impact; and (5) number of ideas generated.[3] But there are also many more, as I can attest from working with innovation chiefs in multiple settings. Some track the total number of experiments conducted in a year; the number of experiments supported by managers; and the degree to which senior leaders are engaged with experiments and have "skin in the game."

At the program level, Intuit uses a lot of metrics company-wide. Within just Zias's own bailiwick of unstructured time, for example, he puts numbers to questions like: "Are people using it? What's the trend? Are people using it over a span of time? Are we getting graduates from unstructured time that are turning into important new offerings? Or are these only supported offerings that move forward?"

Finally, at the level of the individual initiative, metrics must be designed to determine whether it is making appropriate progress, hitting milestone goals, and ultimately delivering the hoped-for value. "Starting from the genesis of an idea," Zias said, a team must have a way of measuring "Is there a customer problem, and what is the problem?"

Zias underscored that Intuit has the advantage of being in the software business; it can track customer behavior to find out if people are getting stuck, if they are looking or not looking to the help pages, if they're finishing, and if they're coming back—as well as if they're getting more in refunds. Each of these becomes a relevant metric.

The Right Metrics for the Job

Deb Sundal leads the part of UnitedHealth Group's innovation system dedicated to supporting intrapreneurs. She told me that performance metrics on her watch have clear functions in three phases: *intake* of new intrapreneurial projects, *design* of those projects, and *realization* of their potential. Figuring out how progress will be measured and reported is one of the most critical tasks of the design phase—yet Sundal finds it is the step that intrapreneurs are most likely to neglect.

The takeaway for Sundal is that part of her team's service to intrapreneurs is to help them think through measurement issues during that crucial design phase—and to consider not only "What should we measure?" but also "Have we communicated with others about what we're measuring? Is there alignment and agreement?" Intrapreneurs are usually eager to move quickly from seeing an opportunity to seizing it, so it is valuable to provide a process for "taking the time to draw alignment across the multiple stakeholders who are either investing, building the teams, or doing the work."

At Tide Spin, VanHimbergen measured success by focusing on the growth of repeat business. "We've been growing week over week. As long as we see growth there, with a lot of early trials coming back and using us again, that's validating our value proposition, which is key to early-stage learning."

If there is one dominant theme cutting across all these examples of how intrapreneurial efforts are assessed, it goes straight back to our theme of learning. Zias, for one, believes strongly in measurement geared toward "evidence of learning." In other words, a team should be able to show that each iteration of its work was smarter than the last, based on feedback received and course corrections in response. At the team level, he wants to see the kind of documentation a scientist conducting an experiment would produce: "Did you have assumptions, and did you lay them out? After you ran experiments, what did you learn?" That record of thinking and discovery becomes great collateral for moving forward, whether the next foray is made by the same team or another one. Zias describes the intelligence gained by well-measured experimentation as "the currency of how our culture works."

At LEGO Group, a company that urgently relies on its

ability to produce a constant stream of new products for a very demanding customer, David Gram, the company's former senior innovation director, said a key lesson from his innovation lab was, "Don't aim to get it right the first time, aim to learn." In an extreme form of this, design teams in the company's Future Lab are given just two weeks to test and iterate a pretotype. That's not a typo—it's an even earlier-stage mockup than a prototype, used to focus collaborative efforts. In these early conversations, "the team constantly feels they are learning new stuff." Then, because the biggest commercialization lessons come when they get it out in the real world, LEGO does market validation through small pilot launches. All along, Gram said, the team measures how much insight and learning they have been able to validate through the various steps and sites.[4]

The implication of all this is that companies that believe in the learning benefits of intrapreneurial efforts find ways of measuring those gains.

So what could be next? Could projects that produce more insight and learning be greenlighted more readily for new phases of work? Could the people behind them be rewarded for that success? Return on intelligence is a conceptual term, but with some effort to attach rigorous and defensible metrics to it, this form of ROI could be calculated with greater precision—and help drive both the change companies want to see throughout their ranks and the innovation that must deliver to grow sustainably. Again, this is why it is so important to get metrics right: they are the most potent reinforcing mechanisms in any effort to influence behavior. Today's companies need to reconcile their old habits of measuring performance with their new goals of supporting intrapreneurial risk-taking. They need to measure return on intelligence.

Learning the Agile Way

Innovation teams have added another core idea to go along with lean startup and design thinking. It's the idea of agile development, and it comes with its own set of methods and metrics. As we discussed initially in chapter 7 with agile, fluid teams, following an agile methodology essentially means that after you embark on an extended effort to create something, you should keep rechecking that your original plan still makes sense based on what you are learning along the way. To recall the words of long-ago general Helmuth von Moltke, "No battle plan ever survives first contact with the enemy." The same goes for innovation: as changes unfold in the broader context of a project and feedback is received from various quarters, it makes sense to adjust the plan based on what you've learned.

Perhaps that doesn't sound radically different—it seems like a pragmatic way to proceed. But most big companies create a blueprint and then build based on it, working heads-down for months, even years, to execute the design. That has traditionally seemed like the quickest and most manageable way to proceed. One where we seldom ever stop or look back to learn.

Agile development gives up that perceived efficiency, because it has teams constantly iterating and reprioritizing, taking one step back in order to take two steps forward. But for all its adjustments, it ends up being more efficient. It avoids that day when a team finishes its work, looks up, and only then discovers that the world has moved on, or the thing they built doesn't really solve an important customer problem. Agile development produces fewer blunders and more valuable solutions in the end because learning is at the center of its process.

What is often called "the agile movement" started in software and has spread into other areas.[5] Deb Sundal at UnitedHealth Group is one of many intrapreneurial leaders who use the term more broadly. "Businesses tend to like the waterfall approach," she said, referring to the traditional software engineering approach in which decisions flow in one direction, cascading from high-level specifications to smaller details. But the lesson to be learned from watching technology developers today is that "you cannot advance innovation in a waterfall approach. It has to be agile."

With the world shifting at every turn to respond to disruption, in software and everywhere else, the agile methodology and its rapid iteration resonate broadly because they achieve a high return on intelligence.

Let a Thousand ~~Failures~~ Learnings Bloom

When managers at UnitedHealth Group went through the exercise of drawing up a mission statement, they specified the enterprise's beliefs and values in five big areas, along with how they translate to people's behaviors. Under the heading of innovation, it pledges: "We will be curious and not afraid to fail in honest efforts to focus on practical and purposeful innovation."

It's the word *fail* that catches my eye. Seldom is it included in such a prominent display of company aspirations. But more businesses should be following suit, because return on intelligence often equates to return on failure.

As we know, most innovation efforts fail at first. Looking specifically at corporate efforts, 2013 research by Harvard's Beth Altringer shows that global intrapreneurial projects fail at least 70 percent of the time.[6] Yet *failure* is much more meaningful

117

than that simple word implies. Bob Schwartz sees plenty of ideas for new products pursued that, while "they don't wind up in the marketplace necessarily," are extremely valuable. "The power of them is that they open a different kind of conversation that didn't exist before." Sometimes they introduce a new concept that is ahead of today's technological capabilities, or they inspire people to push forward into a new domain. For this reason, Ratan Tata, founder of Tata Group, once told the *Economist* that failure is a "gold mine" for a great company.[7] And Honda founder Soichiro Honda declared, "Success is only 1 percent of your work, and the rest—bold overcoming of obstacles. If you are not afraid of obstacles, success will come to you itself."[8]

Indeed, the idea of "embracing failure" has become a mantra in innovation circles. But the point is not really to embrace failure; it's to embrace learning—and to recognize that a huge amount can be learned from failures. A disproved hypothesis is valuable knowledge and produces the next round of effort. So, as Babak Forutanpour puts it, companies should be telling their people: "If you failed trying to build a system with design flaws that should have been obvious, then shame on you. But if you failed at something where something was *learned*, we're actually going to give you a bonus."

There is a reason, of course, that managers would have to be very clear in stating this—and many increasingly are. It goes against eons of experience and expectations. In most people's lives, failures have not been sources of joy; they have been cause for humiliation. This is underlined by a recent survey of corporate employees by Accenture, which found that "although 42 percent consider tolerance of failure from management very important, only one in every eight employees thinks their company is good at that."[9]

In companies that visibly punish failures, you can't blame people for hiding them, even when their hard-won knowledge could help their colleagues. Even if they don't believe they will be penalized for the failure, many don't see the need to communicate what didn't pan out. And if they do understand that value, there isn't often a clear pathway to share what was learned. This isn't a problem limited to business settings; in many realms, when scholars conducting scientific research fail to find what they set out to find, their papers don't get cited or, in many cases, even published. And therefore people keep repeating the effort, going down the same paths that look promising but turn out to be dead ends.

More recently, there has been a trend toward companies visibly doing the opposite of punishing failures: they have started to celebrate them—and better yet, to reframe them as learning. Intuit, for example, coaches teams to see disproven hypotheses as a success and learning event. "The only true failure is failure to learn," says Intuit innovation leader Jeff Zias, "so we began coaching teams to learn fast, to gather disproven or proven hypotheses as learnings, and to consider every form of fast learning a success." Tata Group has an annual competition with a prize for the best failed idea, showing Ratan Tata's belief in failure being valuable—a gold mine for a company. BMW was an early advocate of celebrating failure, having honored its first "flop of the year" decades ago. And maybe the first company to start throwing parties for failed projects was W. L. Gore, maker of GORE-TEX fabric. As strange as these celebrations may sound, they have the powerful effect of signaling that behaviors like problem-finding, problem-solving, self-correction, and smart risk-taking are admirable—and are so needed that they should be held up as models even when they fall short of their goals.

More than that, the competitive nature of a "best failure" award has the benefit of making people think harder about what separates better flops from worse ones. A failed plan deserves to be celebrated, for example, if it accidentally achieves something unexpected (like the well-known accidental discoveries of Post-it Notes and Viagra). And a project deserves to be celebrated if its unhoped-for results wound up steering efforts down a more productive path. But a failure does not deserve to be celebrated if it did not create knowledge that hadn't existed before. And it certainly doesn't deserve to be celebrated if, even after its failure becomes evident, it refuses to die.

On this last point, Google has a special honor it bestows on those who understood when to stop working on something and pulled the plug on it. As Salim Ismail told me about it, he underscored how valuable this is. Typically, a lot of good money is thrown after bad or souring initiatives just because people don't want their names associated with terminated or "failed" projects. In classic Silicon Valley style, Alphabet X (the research and development lab formerly know as Google X) has a high-ranking manager with the job title of "Captain of Moonshots," whose job it is to develop big-thinking projects. His name is Astro Teller, and the moonshots he's seeking are radically new answers to real-life problems. Other companies might benefit from how Teller thinks about incentives for innovation. He advocates granting ownership stakes, or "upside" in other forms, to the leaders of projects with bigger risk/reward profiles. But he also believes in giving people more reason to say when something isn't working. In some cases, this means actual bonuses to teams who have admitted, "We spent the last year on this, but we're done. We're dead. All the data says no." At one postmortem party, he physically put a project in its "grave" and summed up the lessons learned from it in an epitaph.[10] According to Ismail, "When people heard about that, it gave them more confidence that they could pursue long-shot opportunities, and their failure, if that's how things turned out, would not be punished."

It will be interesting in the years to come to observe whether these failure awards continue to proliferate, and whether the companies celebrating them see growing numbers of project teams self-nominating themselves for the distinction. Wayne Morris at SAP told me that the Silicon Valley mantra of "Fail early, fail often" is often repeated around him, but he said, "Personally, I don't like the way it's phrased." He prefers to talk in terms of discovering what won't work. Dr. Vishal Sikka, formerly of SAP, seems to agree. In an interview with the *Financial Times* about how SAP celebrates failure, he explained, "At the end of every cycle, we do an 'I wish/I like' session. 'I like' is the things that went right; and 'I wish' are the things we wish we'd done differently." This, he believes, is the way to achieve "continuous, rapid innovation, learning from failures, with the failure of a project not being equated with the failure of a person."[11] This is similar to what we do with our clients. For example, after we've run an experiment, we capture each stakeholder's "what we liked" and "what we would do differently." Along with various metrics, capturing and synthesizing this kind of feedback helps define a clear path to move forward—or not to move forward at all.

Zias at Intuit is another manager who likes twisting things around to be about "the speed of learning." If an intrapreneur says to him, "We were so stupid—the thing we did completely failed," he quickly turns the conversation around and says, "I think what you've done is just quickly disproven your hypothesis—which is awesome."

That type of encouragement keeps people innovating. The

more they innovate, the more they learn—and that learning guides the success of future moonshots. This virtuous circle only works when we connect the loop between intrapreneurship and learning. But how?

DIY Playbook—Maximize Return on Intelligence

Intrapreneurs rely on constant learning in an open, agile environment where the culture can balance structure with autonomy and metrics with flexibility as part of these DIY principles:

1. When in Doubt, Test It Out
2. Make Learning a Priority
3. Measure Return on Intelligence
4. Make Failure Feasible

1. When in Doubt, Test It Out

Experiment to learn quickly and efficiently. We've seen numerous strategies for fast and frugal idea testing—starting with asset-based thinking, trial and error, small bets, and more. Reddit cofounders Alexis Ohanian and Steve Huffman were "just two dudes in a room" with "no idea what they were doing"—but they learned fast through iteration. Starting with no-frills, frugal bets helps you learn and pivot faster using fewer resources. This approach takes the sting away from failure and allows you to build on success.

Pretotype and prototype. LEGO's pretotype and other ways to build simple proofs of concept enable fast and frugal testing with props that people can pick up and pass around.

Let go of assumptions. The DIY ethos requires a clean-slate policy, including bypassing confirmation bias (looking for evidence to support your existing assumption) in order to remain open to new insight. It's important, as well, to avoid premature debate, waiting until you have facts and data from field tests before using teams to pull ideas apart.

2. Make Learning a Priority

Create a learning competency. Learning yields growth and innovation, vastly advances our strategic understanding of business, and helps us avoid repeating mistakes and doubling back down dead ends. As mentioned earlier, Stanley Black & Decker's business model experiments in fast-paced emerging markets allowed them to test ideas that otherwise would have been rolled out in large-scale pilots. The repeatable process enabled multiple iterations and adjustments at low to no cost—saving money and drawing insights early, before a massive rollout was required. In essence, they built a learning competency through active practice and by adding inquiry into their everyday work.

Learn from stakeholders. The initial public versions of Twitter and Foursquare were flawed, but they used customer data to improve and become successful. Learning occurs faster when we put ourselves in the path of other people. Traditionally, this meant a one-way exchange of information from teachers, experts, or anyone with formal authority. Intrapreneurs understand that learning emerges through interactions with *any* stakeholder group, although the most valuable source of business insight is often customers. (Intrapreneurs are frequently in front-line or external-facing positions.) Learning occurs, as well, by participating in diverse teams, by connecting with industry colleagues, and by seeking out specialized expertise within your own organization.

Don't get overly attached to ideas. Intrapreneurs let go of assumptions and overturn ideas they may have considered to be fact in the past. I tell would-be innovators: be ready to let the data disprove your theories. This mind-set leaves them open to disruptive thinking and gets them accustomed to finding new ways to validate hunches.

Create a culture that values learning. Intuit, Google, and GE Healthcare are established innovators because they make inquiry and innovation high priorities from the top down and bottom up. As we see in these organizations, leaders need to reward ingenuity and build it into the central mission of the enterprise. In addition, because the effort is all about advancement, organizations need to take risks to make leaps in learning.

Remove structural obstacles by creating a clear approach for innovation. Give intrapreneurs the time and space they need to proceed. According to Larry Keeley, that means "enough time to produce an actual concept—which can be an intensive freed-up period of about three to four weeks—plus a center of excellence to fully support and assist their effort."

3. Measure Return on Intelligence

Connect learning to results. Use appropriate metrics to manage goals and show success in generating learning. This approach to learning creates a discipline around intrapreneurship, thereby legitimizing it and opening up a path for internal innovation.

Create flexible metrics. Simply put, metrics are powerful drivers of innovation. Measures and key performance metrics (KPIs) may need to be newly created expressly to support return on intelligence. One senior manager proposes "setting up metrics that foster innovative behavior, champion openness to new ideas, and challeng[e] the status quo." Other elements, such as small wins, early-stage testing, customer validation, upvotes from colleagues, and even simply posing ideas that test the status quo can all be measured as part of a new set of metrics to help intrapreneurs gain momentum.

Scale insight. One positive by-product of measurement is the data it generates. At Tide Spin, the team measured the growth of repeat business to find signs of success. Sharing data widely helps scale insights, institutionalize learning, and generate a record of intrapreneurial projects and the output they have produced.

4. Make Failure Feasible

Empower people to pull the plug. Individual intrapreneurs should make the call about when to pivot or end a pilot. (Clear metrics for return on intelligence remove guesswork from the equation.) This level of trust minimizes stigma from failure, preserves passion, and encourages intrapreneurs to use what they learn to discover a more feasible solution.

Reward failure. Alphabet's Astro Teller said: "People will do profoundly amazing things if you set the social norms correctly. It's those social norms and actually reinforcing them . . . That's what unlocks innovation."[12] Making failure a social norm creates a culture that encourages experiments as opposed to penalizing and personalizing failure. Even more, finding ways to reward failure increases learning dramatically. That is why Intuit, Google, BMW, and W. L. Gore commemorate their "best" failures with awards that celebrate risk-taking and encourage problem-solving.

Reframe failure as learning. Failure carries too much baggage for some organizations. In these cases, rather than trying to overcome a deeply embedded aversion to failure, it's best to simply reframe failure as learning. As Blood Orange collaborator Sam Reid told us, "We've found it more useful to just call the outcome of whatever we do 'learning.' When we do well, it's learning. When we don't, it's learning."

Turn failure into value. Babak Forutanpour says that companies should want you to fail, as long as you fail at something where a lesson was learned. Expressly separating and elevating "valuable" flops from useless ones helps organizations recognize when failed attempts generate learning, create knowledge, and send innovators down a new and potentially profitable path.

Scale learning from failure. Use after-action review to analyze failure and make adjustments based on what you've learned. Target, for one, "follows the learnings" by using them to do things differently. Some organizations tell stories of major failure to make them memorable and to help create a narrative with lessons the rest of the organization can learn; others use innovation management software to track how and when insights are shared, as well as how many views these insights elicit.

Executive Scorecard:

- How do you encourage learning across the organization?
- Are learning, insight, and experimentation expressly infused within your culture?
- Is experimentation a clear and express part of your innovation strategy?
- Do you have metrics that measure and manage learning and sharing intelligence?
- Is failure a part of the accepted social norms of the enterprise?
- How do you reward the "best" failures or learnings and scale these insights?

EIGHT

Principle 6: Create the Commons

Seema Patel is a leader in one of the many labs I've studied that are devoted to supporting innovation within large organizations—in her case, the federal agency USAID. As is often the case with leaders like Patel, her background includes an intrapreneurial stint. Back in 2007, she was working as a consultant to USAID when a newly appointed administrator, Henrietta Fore, arrived and started using an unfamiliar term. Fore was saying the agency should create "the commons," or a space where information is openly shared, for the whole development community. At first, Patel recalled, "We didn't know what she was talking about." But by 2008, when the initiative was launched, Patel was helping lead the charge, as the manager of a team of three.

The notion was to create an online platform and program

where citizens, NGOs, government ministries, philanthropic donors, farmers, health-care workers, businesses—basically, anyone with a stake in development—could come together to share data and ideas, ask questions and get answers, and form collaborative partnerships. An early announcement promised it would be a space "owned by no one," where a user could "find the best way to plant and harvest cassava, communicate with a donor organization that will fund experts in building trade capacity, and check the price Kraft Inc. paid Guatemalan small-holder farmers last month for 100 pounds of shade-grown coffee."[1] It was an incredibly ambitious vision, and despite the team's tiny size, they were determined to make it happen. "We had very little money to do it," Patel said, "but we had good ideas about creating experiences, and processes, and opportunities for creative thinking." They also had incredibly diverse networks.

The fact that they pulled it off goes a long way to explain Patel's enduring conviction that intrapreneurship succeeds best when it is "open and inclusive." This was an initiative aimed at making USAID's development work itself more open and inclusive, bringing in new voices and innovators, and the team built that capability in exactly that way. They started by saying, "All right, let's convene some of the people that we think have interesting, unique, and diverse ideas" about aggregation sites, virtual communities, and behavior. Their method was to create *the Commons*, or "a space where a diversity of ideas and perspectives could be brought together and everyone could start thinking more creatively about what they can achieve."

In the decade since, Patel's focus at the Global Development Lab has been to support innovators and entrepreneurs from outside the organization as well as innovators and intrapreneurs inside the organization, working across the agency's far-flung work sites to develop their ideas and mainstream the ones that prove most effective. As she and her staff talk to intrapreneurs about taking their solutions to scale, "we talk about this team concept a lot," she said—and "when we say a team, we mean thinking in concentric circles. Not just the core team, but then, who are your 'friends and family' that you can prototype with to get those quick feedback loops? And then: Who's your broader team, in the bigger system and environment? And how do you engage leadership to be excited about what you're doing and want to be part of it?" They impress upon people that "intrapreneurship flourishes where there are diverse teams that bring together different capabilities, mind-sets, experiences." Patel summed things up: "That, to me, is a key aspect of intrapreneurship. Being able to collect those people."

The Global Development Lab has four guiding principles, which include their determination to be evidence based, catalytic, and agile. But would it surprise you to hear what tops the list? You guessed it: "open and inclusive."

THE SHIFT: CREATE THE COMMONS

From	To
Exclusive "white coat" projects	Enlisting cross-functional teammates across the organization
Staying inside the organization	Partnering broadly to rapidly acquire knowledge and accelerate growth
Design by the internal experts	Engaging in codesign with customers, peers, and outside partners

Why Full Inclusion Is So Important

A call for openness and inclusion sounds about as controversial as praising parenthood and apple pie. But we need to get past the call for action and truly execute this crucial competency. When I work with corporations to instill intrapreneurship-driven innovation, inclusion shows up more in the talk and much less in the walk. Yet the payback gained when we involve many more types of people, and thinking, in the innovation process is enormous and just as diverse as the people and perspectives we want installed on these teams.

Better Ideas

First, greater openness and inclusion generate better thinking about innovations. This is something I have heard many creative people observe, but for sheer enthusiasm it would be hard to beat Philippe Mauldin, who saw the power of combining diverse groups at Fidelity Labs: "Let's just start with putting people on a team that have different skills," he said. "Say, a project manager versus a design thinker—I mean, even before you get to gender, ethnicity, and experience, they're coming at this from totally different angles! You've got a project manager who's all about market opportunities paired with someone who's the customer advocate. Can I tell you, there's nothing more beautiful than watching the two of them work together."

Mauldin went on to describe how, with each new addition to the mix—technical expert, editor, experienced entrepreneur, representative of a particular generation or demographic background—another point of view is brought to the table and the group's thinking becomes far more creative. "I've drunk the Kool-Aid on that one," he said, then summed up, "There's probably nothing more important in innovation than diversity on teams."

3M's chief design officer, Eric Quint, says that such diverse collaboration is critical to his organization's long-term success. "Fundamental to the success of our design organization is what I call 'collaborative creativity', ensuring that our team is constantly engaged in vibrant idea exchange across disciplines, to accelerate the path toward new and sustainable 3M solutions."[2]

Fidelity's and 3M's belief in combining many minds is based on its own experience, but the idea also has ample support in scholarly research. One oft-cited study used a controlled experimental approach to compare two groups' performance on a brainstorming task—one group was made up wholly of Anglo-Americans and the other group combined Anglo-Americans, Anglo-Asians, African Americans, and Hispanic Americans. It found that the ethnically diverse group produced ideas of higher quality.[3] Quite recently, another study of corporations' publicly available information looked for a link between policies that promote more pro-diversity cultures (specifically regarding women and minorities) and greater "innovation efficiency"— that is, numbers of new product announcements, patents, and patent citations generated per R&D dollar. Sure enough, it found that link, leading the authors to conclude that "a wider range of views, backgrounds, and expertise can help innovative problem solving, and a culture of inclusion may help attract and retain talent."[4]

More Ideas

A good way to wind up with better ideas is, well, to start with more of them. Inclusion serves this goal directly, and that explains why so many companies are trying to democratize innovation. L'Oréal, for example, has an annual contest called Beauty Shakers, which showcases clever new solutions devised by teams at any level and in any part of the company. Winners are crowned in three categories: sustainability, "out of the box" innovation, and overall excellence. (The last, as top prize, is reserved for ideas that have been implemented and are contributing to the bottom line.) A good example of a recent winner is Christa Rowland's team, which spotted a way to make a fairly simple change in the manufacturing process for lip gloss that would both save the company money and reduce its environmental impact. By figuring out how to keep mixing tanks free of residue, Rowland's team cut out a cleaning step in the process that had not only delayed production of every batch but required the use of cleaning chemicals and hundreds of thousands of liters of water. The team's ingenuity gave it the chance to present in front of a judging committee, including CEO Frédéric Rozé, and ultimately to be awarded the $20,000 top prize at L'Oréal's Year End Business Review in New York City.[5]

The point of high-visibility awards like this is not just to reward intrapreneurial achievement—it is to encourage more of it. When I talked with people at L'Oréal, Beauty Shakers had been going on for several years and more than thirty projects had already materialized from it, from a new mobile app that allows someone to use the mirror function on their phone to virtually "try on" different cosmetics (Makeup Genius), to an appetizing retail display for nail polishes (Ultimate Essie Candy Bar) that significantly boosted sales, to a customer relationship management (CRM) database solution thought to be the first focused on luxury goods buyers.

I'll mention more programs below, all designed to spur more intrapreneurial efforts throughout organizations. For the moment, let the general point suffice. When management makes it clear that it really wants to see and celebrate innovation at all levels by all people, the innovations start to pile up.

Broader Commitment

Whatever ideas emerge from an intrapreneurial effort, they are sure to go further if more people have a sense of buy-in and feel committed to seeing them through. Decades of change management research and experience have established that involving more stakeholders early on in identifying problems and seeking solutions leads to easier implementation later and ultimately more positive impact.

This is a point that applies broadly to firms' needs for innovation and also translates to specific advice for teams. Deb Sundal is adamant about it. She makes a point to urge intrapreneurial teams to behave inclusively from the start. "There are hundreds of thousands of brilliant people sitting around this organization," she says, "[and] if you are responsible for developing a new concept, you own the curation of many, many, many minds."

Innovators shouldn't make the mistake of thinking they can hole up in a garage and build out an idea and then have everyone say "Wow" on the day it is unveiled. Sundal emphasizes that people are more likely to say, "Ooh, I like that" when they recognize that their thoughts and learnings are in the design. Active coaching helps in this area, Sundal believes, because intrapreneurs "are really great subject-matter experts, but they don't harness the immense resources that are available at their fingertips." Many need advice on reaching out to "those thought leaders across the organization who actually have very smart opinions" on their solution, and then later coming back to those people to say, "Let me show you where I am." It can be tricky, given the danger of erring on the other side and getting caught in "the trap of death by consensus," as Sundal puts it.

The idea is not to blunt the point of the project but to sharpen it. Someday, when the innovation reaches "a product stage gate and it's going to be scaled—[and] someone could say, 'Well, they didn't think about x, y, and z,'" Sundal knows that an open and inclusive approach can make that objection far less likely.

Talent Development

Making intrapreneurial opportunities from ideation to experimentation widely available to all is a priceless employee retention and leadership development opportunity.

As one participant in SAP's Run Your Idea program put it: "The main thing is that we have end-to-end responsibility, starting from the ideation to the point of checking and verifying with customers, to finally implementing the solution and making it as a business." Another participant added: "It doesn't matter, actually, whether you win or not. The training that they provide you, the mentor support, the coaching—that's just a great growth opportunity, in any stage of your career."[6] Taking charge of bringing some new and valuable thing into existence, which involves many moving parts and which must ultimately succeed in a competitive market, is perhaps the very best way to learn how to lead.

Two important questions follow from this. First: What if the leadership lessons that intrapreneurs soak

BARRIERS TO CREATING THE COMMONS

- Need to get beyond your "usual suspects" / core innovators
- Turf wars can create conflict
- Easy to envision, difficult to execute without a thoughtful process and strategy

up fail to emphasize the kind of open and inclusive outreach that Deb Sundal describes—in that case, would they be adequately prepared to take on greater leadership responsibilities in a twenty-first-century global enterprise? And second: What happens if the population of intrapreneurs a company recognizes and supports is itself not inclusive—for example, if it is overwhelmingly made up of white men with EVP in their title?

If leading an intrapreneurial project is a good way to acquire leadership skills and broad-based knowledge of the enterprise, then the mix of intrapreneurs a company cultivates should reflect the mix it hopes to see in its future top management ranks.

Who to Include? (Hint: Everyone)

Some enterprises go beyond extending the *invitation* to everyone to innovate and instead try to create the *expectation* that they will do so. Wayne Morris told me that, "[At SAP] we understand that successful businesses require multiple approaches to innovation, and we're trying to change the corporate culture . . . to include employee-driven or grassroots-type innovation." Most big companies have tended to "drive innovation top down," but SAP is convinced that augmenting this traditional approach by adding employee-driven innovation, along with internal and external startups, fosters many more valuable opportunities.

The basic question SAP and others are raising is: Who owns innovation around here? And the answer many are arriving at is: everyone. But to put a slightly finer point on things, companies should aim for full-range participation along a number of different dimensions.

All Levels and Functions

The big shift in corporate innovation is that it has moved out of the narrow control of leadership and beyond the particular skill sets of the research and development department. Any program to achieve greater inclusion should make it clear that people from the manufacturing shop floor to the headquarters top floor can be sources of new value creation. At Disney, the idea to open retail Disney stores in shopping malls was an idea that came from the rank and file. At W. L. Gore, it was a medical device engineer working on heart implant technology who spotted a way to make a better guitar string. Gore's long-lasting Elixir strings are now the best-selling product in their category.[7]

Intuit is adamant about this highly democratized approach, as CEO Brad Smith makes clear. "We are a thirty-year-old, eight-thousand-employee startup," he said. "All eight thousand employees are entrepreneurs and they're innovators. It's everybody's job to create, to invent, and to look for new and better ways to improve our customers' lives."

The benefit is even greater if people know they do not have to stay in their lanes as they think about what the business could do better. If someone in accounting has an idea relating to customer service, there should be a pathway for it to be expressed and taken seriously—even if that person will not ultimately own the responsibility to develop it. Of course, most ideas people have relate directly to what they see and think about in their everyday jobs, but signaling that they should not let their imaginations go further is asking for only incremental improvements.

Marc Nager of TechStars points to the roots of that constraint: "Go to most major business schools or any universities with undergraduate and graduate programs and look around. They have buildings very specifically labeled—the engineering building, the art building, the music, business, and science buildings." When you carve up an organization in this way, he notes that "you silo people—and you're limiting the interactions and the potential flow of ideas." The best ideas, he said, emerge from a "primordial soup" of different and often conflicting beliefs, desires, and ways of knowing all mixed together. Impose too much order to focus people's activity and "all of a sudden you take away some of the primary elements you need for that level of creativity."

Babak Forutanpour, who started the FLUX inventor groups inside Qualcomm, said, "What's interesting is literally half the people in FLUX weren't even engineers in the areas that they were discussing. . . . They couldn't build it if they wanted to." It's hard to argue with the level of inclusion FLUX was able to achieve by welcoming ideas from all quarters. Foruntanpour's original group of eight fellow conspirators grew dramatically into an intrapreneurial movement of three thousand employees, generating hundreds of inventive ideas and patents.

All Demographics and Ages

Along with greater participation from people outside the classic "innovation" functions of the business, companies benefit by inviting ideas from employees with different backgrounds. The focus on diversity that many originally adopted as a "social responsibility" or demographic necessity is now being recognized as a key to ongoing growth and high performance. As one scholarly paper put it, "The innovative and creative potential inherent to a diverse workforce (in terms of ethnic origin, nationality, cultural background, religion, gender, age, education, lifestyle, working style, way of thinking, etc.) can be used to bridge cultural boundaries and search for original problem solutions, innovative product ideas, and targeted marketing initiatives."[8] In other words, diversity can become a competitive advantage.

At the level of self-forming teams, this is something to be encouraged, even if it can't be strictly imposed. Intrapreneurial teams usually require more than usual levels of esprit de corps; they are groups that not only click in the office but would be happy hanging out together after work. Conscripting teammates with very different backgrounds and perspectives can sometimes complicate the creativity that comes from spontaneity.

Forutanpour told me a story of his early, ill-fated effort to engineer more diversity into a FLUX team. He remembered saying to a colleague, "For your team, let's really mix things up— let's try to get the most diverse crowd we can." But he found that their "little petri dish" didn't work out—in fact, the team "imploded." Forutanpour is a big advocate of diverse teams, but he believes that the magic happens organically. "If everyone looks and acts like you, it's boring," he insisted, "and some people like that safety, but not innovators." Yet he understands that forcing diversity can backfire. "Folks should be different enough to challenge each other's assumptions, but like each other enough that they would have a beer together after work."

Members need to have a basis to form productive relationships, and that usually happens on its own. Inclusion is another opportunity to provide guidelines, guardrails, and other loose infrastructure—as long as there's flexibility built in. With that, teams can benefit from the creativity that comes with diversity while retaining its ability to pull together ad hoc to get the job done.

Outsiders as Well as Insiders

In a book focused on internal disruption and intrapreneurship, it may seem out of scope to touch on the ways companies are including complete outsiders in the processes of hatching and incubating ideas. Yet this trend—which covers everything from investing in startups to co-creating with customers to crowdsourcing ideas through grand challenges—is a big part of the story in corporate innovation and often represents an alternative to looking to one's own workforce for ideas. In other words, it's yet another attempt to bolster inclusion and diversity.

Still, for every idea that is hatched outside a company, there needs to be an internal champion to make sure it gains traction. At the casual restaurant chain Buffalo Wild Wings, for example, it was a group of franchisees who cooked up the company's most successful promotion—putting timers on tables at lunchtime, with a promise that if meals didn't arrive within fifteen minutes they would be free.[9] At LEGO, customers are a big part of innovation, submitting designs through a "LEGO Ideas" website for new sets the company could sell—and when their ideas are accepted, even receiving royalties. In both companies, the innovations have succeeded because there were also employees who were excited about them and capable of taking them to scale.

Most importantly, looking to the outside is part of how successful intrapreneurs themselves operate as they enlist the help they need to make headway with their ideas. Deutsche Telekom's UQBATE acceleration program, mentioned in chapter 5, makes clear that the intrapreneurial community it wants to convene goes beyond employees. Under the heading of "Whom we are looking for," its website lists three categories of contributors:

- We are looking for *colleagues with ideas* for new business—apart from today's core business. They should be passionate about new ideas and business and should have the time and energy to act as project lead to make their ideas come true.
- We are looking for *colleagues who do not have ideas* themselves but have a serious interest in joining another team of intrapreneurs to make their ideas come true. They should be passionate about new ideas and business and should have the time and energy to act as co-founder or project-member to realize these ideas.

And . . .

- We are looking for *external partners* to support our teams with their know-how and experience. We are especially looking for designers and developers to support our internal startup teams.[10]

Outsourcing and open innovation, in other words, are not the black-and-white contrast to employee-led efforts that they might seem to be. Bringing in ideas and efforts from people who aren't company employees can be just another step along the continuum of open and inclusive intrapreneurship.

DIY Playbook—Create the Commons

The idea that intrapreneurship should be open and inclusive should not surprise anyone. Still, we are left with the question of how to achieve that goal. My approach throughout this book has been to hold up principles to help you create your own DIY playbook. That approach reflects the realities that (a) best practices are forever changing, and (b) the "best" answers will, in any case, never come down to cookie-cutter solutions but will be customized to particular settings. With that in mind, start your playbook with these field-tested, flexible ideas for inclusive intrapreneurship:

1. Plan for Full Inclusion
2. Make It Safe to Innovate
3. Use Technology in Appropriate Measure
4. Train Future Intrapreneurs
5. Create Porous Networks

1. Plan for Full Inclusion

Signal inclusion clearly. Every person is a potential innovator and solutions can come from any corner of an ecosystem. Innovation programs that signal this loud and clear serve their enterprises well. Programs that transmit the opposite message—that innovation is best left to isolated parts of the organization, or to people from certain backgrounds or with certain cognitive strengths—put severe limits on what can be achieved.

Remember cognitive diversity. Research clearly demonstrates that getting the most creative solutions is most certainly about identity diversity (background, experience, gender, race, and culture), and it's also about cognitive diversity. Bringing people together who have varied experiences and expertise can unleash true breakthrough ideas. In other words, getting data scientists in a room with daycare workers may be just what you need to address, say, the rising cost of higher education.

Create an inviting space. If you build the right sandbox, intrapreneurs from all over the organization will dive into it.

Create space and structure for intrapreneurship and you will keep your most creative people engaged. You will also see the quality and quantity of homegrown innovations increase. And you may discover that many of the people who are most capable of forging the future of your enterprise don't look like the ones who forged its past.

2. Make It Safe to Innovate

Take baby steps. There's a lot to be said for inviting people to innovate by keeping the bar for commitment low for the first leap. Innovation challenges, hackathons, and general calls for ideas, for instance, don't necessarily make huge claims on people's time or require massive amounts of confidence on their part.

Parse up projects. Not everyone with a good idea is able or eager to run with it. Someone who spots an opportunity might only be willing to commit a weekend or a few hours to articulating it. That shouldn't mean that the idea has no chance to be heard. Creating a well-defined innovation path means these ideas can be connected to others who are more likely to execute a validated idea.

Remove some of the risk. Gifford Pinchot III, who coined the term *intrapreneur*, said: "To become an intrapreneur, an individual must risk something of value to himself."[11] Luckily, in a large organization, that risk is almost never the kind of financial stake that an entrepreneur has in a venture. In this case, risk has more to do with potential wasted time and possibly the reputational damage of being attached to a "failure." At its worst, it could lead to getting pushed out of the organization. Without removing that personal risk altogether, companies need to find ways to dial it down in order to induce more employees to behave intrapreneurially.

Create psychological safety. At the team level, the most important concept to be discussed in recent years is the need for "psychological safety" in group interactions.[12] Many people were introduced to this line of thinking by an influential *New York Times Magazine* article titled "What Google Learned from Its Quest to Build the Perfect Team."[13] It details how the tech giant used analytics to sift through data about the activities, attitudes, and achievements of 180 teams over two years to arrive at the handful of traits the best of them shared. Among the discoveries was that members had a sense of psychological safety, meaning they could let down their guard in team meetings and voice opinions or raise questions they would suppress in other settings where the risk of judgment or other repercussions was higher.

At Fidelity, Sean Belka talked about the importance of making Fidelity Labs "a safe space for experimentation." Seema Patel of USAID told me, "I believe that intrapreneurship flourishes where there are diverse teams that bring together different capabilities, mind-sets, experiences—but where there is also psychological safety [and] alignment of incentives around an opportunity." Comments like these hint at what more and more research demonstrates: that a central innovation function can help drive sustainable innovation by creating awareness of the concept and providing training to intrapreneurial leaders.

3. Use Technology in Appropriate Measure

Look at low-tech for high impact. At Qualcomm, when Babak Forutanpour decided to spread his idea of invention-oriented lunch groups, he did it in a decidedly low-tech way. He taped up posters in hallways, designed to appeal to the problem-solvers he suspected were all around him. One version had a picture of a USB stick, another of a showerhead, and another of a line of dominoes.

"If you can improve on this," the headlines read, "we want to talk to you." This simple start grew his grassroots innovation group from a handful to three thousand in a matter of months.

Make it "social." This kind of outreach has become easier and can go further with the advent of "social enterprise" tools. Spigit, for example, is a software platform some companies use for crowdsourcing ideas from people throughout an enterprise. UnitedHealth Group has deployed it as part of a program called ignite! Innovation. After piloting a few time-boxed idea challenges with particular teams and figuring out how to manage the related communications, idea refinement processes, and other implementation issues, it ran a company-wide challenge in which the CEO called for ideas for reducing health-care costs. More than a thousand ideas poured in when the program kicked off in 2011, and more than three thousand people participated by proposing or responding to them. Once people gained familiarity with the platform, it became easy for teams at every level of the company to use it, to the point that hundreds more challenges have been launched at UnitedHealth Group since.

4. Train Future Intrapreneurs

Create a structured approach. Larry Keeley of Doblin reminded me that innovation initiatives can be made more sustainable by providing "superior tradecraft" to innovators on the inside. Deutsche Telekom's program UQBATE, mentioned earlier, guides employees through a structured innovation process that begins with a boot camp for idea generation, then proceeds quickly to interacting with real customers, building prototypes, and iterating to the point of beta-testing working products. The final decisions about whether to shut down or move forward with an initiative are made jointly with the intrapreneurs. While the company sees this structured approach as a way to accelerate the launch of innovative offerings, and has seen many turn into revenue-producers, a big part of the rationale for putting hundreds of people through this multimonth process is that it not only wants next-generation products—it wants to grow the next generation of intrapreneurial talent.

Create inclusion through incubation. Numerous intrapreneurs in training have worked on projects at Microsoft's Garage, an incubator the company established in 2009. In 2014, it reported that roughly 3,300 Microsoft employees had worked on more than ten thousand different projects developing "everything from robotic arms to a motion-sensor-controlled LED wall to a data-visualization video where all the bugs from a team's past year of releases were represented as aliens being shot down by laser cannon."[14] Again, the message sent by broad inclusion is that innovation is something learnable and not to be left to some brainiac few.

Use active mentoring. One of the best forms of risk management a company can provide to its intrapreneurs is active mentoring. A good mentor doesn't make risk go away or shelter a project from it in any direct way, but instead helps the team learn how to understand and mitigate it—which is essential learning they will take to future projects. Thus, mentors aren't usually the same people who provide air cover for projects. They are people who themselves have succeeded as intrapreneurs or entrepreneurs and have wisdom to impart that isn't necessarily found in a corporation's upper managerial ranks.

At Intuit, intrapreneurs are not left alone to sink or swim. In fact, the company has a number of individuals whose entire job is coaching and encouraging project teams. On top of that, the organization has created a network of "innovation catalysts"—capable mentors who choose to spend 10 percent of their work time guiding other employees working on innovation initiatives, especially by helping them learn and adhere to design thinking principles.[15] Finally, because managers at Intuit have explicit incentives to recognize and support entrepreneurial behavior and experimentation, mentoring arises naturally within the organization.

5. Create Porous Networks

Integrate your ecosystems. It is vital for intrapreneurial teams to move across silos and matrices to connect with other parts of a company's ecosystem, such as supply chain partners, customers, service providers, franchisees, startups, and more—especially if their innovations involve emerging technologies or other new realms of knowledge.

Network with entrepreneurial startups. Many intrapreneurs forge connections to the world of startups as they see entrepreneurial ventures trying to solve the same or related problems. Target, for example, has held open competitions for retail technology solution startups, which give the startups the opportunity to win some financial backing while Target gets to know them and watch them work. Lowe's makes it known to outside solution developers that its physical store network offers a real-world testing environment—for example, to try out customer-assisting robots or virtual reality showrooms. Marc Nager of Telluride Venture Accelerator and cofounder of Startup Weekend told me about Sprint Corporation's extensive outreach to startups and their conviction that "innovation is a lot about leveraging the knowledge and the talent not just inside the corporation but creating that porous wall for us to share our ideas and vice versa."

Have an "outside-in" approach. Mike Steep, executive director of Stanford University's Disruptive Technology program, which focuses on disruptive technologies, told me that not many intrapreneurs inside corporations have had the chance in their corporate careers to learn the art of building external network connections. Steep became aware of this during his tenure at Microsoft and PARC, the latter being the legendary R&D arm of Xerox that now does custom research for other companies. From that vantage point, he noticed that the most successful intrapreneurs were the ones who had ways of finding out about technologies emerging from other sectors and organizations outside their own companies—and sometimes outside their own industries—and who were quick to consider how those technologies might apply to their own customers' problems. He calls this an "outside-in" approach, contrasting to the "inside-out" mode of starting with a company's legacy products and seeking new markets for them with using a company's existing expertise to solve new customer problems, creating entirely new products.

Executive Scorecard

- Are you a champion for diversity and full inclusion?
- In what ways do you use inclusion and diversity as a competitive advantage?
- Have you created space and structure for DIY innovation to develop widely and flourish within your organization?
- Do people at all levels feel safe to propose ideas, experiment, and develop innovation teams?
- How do you keep intrapreneurship from being exclusive

to R&D in your enterprise and keep innovation free from silos?

- Do you look at inclusion and diversity through multiple lenses: identity diversity such as age, race and ethnicity, gender, and so forth cognitive diversity, such as experience and thinking style?

NINE

Principle 7: Engage Passion and Purpose

What can a parent do when he learns that his child has a chronic disease such as type 1 diabetes? If you are like Lane Desborough, you don't wait passively for progress in medical science—you connect with others who are like-minded, and you start working toward new solutions.

Type 1 diabetes renders the pancreas incapable of producing the insulin necessary to shift glucose out of the bloodstream and into cells, where it can be converted into energy. Without insulin, blood-sugar levels spike and the body can't get the nourishment it needs to survive. When his son, Hayden, was diagnosed with the disease in 2009, Desborough was a product manager at GE Energy, applying his training in process control chemical engineering to the efficient operation of oil refineries. While he had never worked anywhere near health care, he began to see that the whole-system approach required for diabetes management had some similarities to chemical plant management. As he recalls now, "I was working on the world's energy problem, but my passion and empathy were driving me in another direction altogether."

Like so many others living with diabetes care, he stayed awake late into the night managing his son's blood sugar, check-ing and adjusting every few hours. A question occurred to him very early on. At a time when so many sensors and networks were being equipped to "talk" to each other via the expanding "internet of things," why was he stuck using devices that com-municated poorly—or not at all—with each other? In a world increasingly populated by "smart" things, why was diabetes-related medical equipment so dumb?

Before long, Desborough left GE to join medical device firm Medtronic, and within months he was leading the engineering team commercializing an "adaptive cruise control" system to partially automate insulin delivery. As an intrapreneurial leader within the company, he framed the objective as much bigger than selling a product. He told an interviewer in 2011 that his aspira-tion was to deliver improved outcomes, which he put into three categories: reducing glycemic variability, increasing lifestyle flex-ibility, and reducing therapy effort. "I tend to look at how various products and services can work together as a system to provide these outcomes," he said, implying that his prior engineering training was important to his success. But there was something else driving it, too, he recognized: "The fact that I go home every night and *experience* glycemic variability, lifestyle constraints, and therapy effort, as part of a family with diabetes, helps me focus my engineering efforts to improve these outcomes."[1]

That personal drive kept Desborough making connections

with the diabetes community on every level. When I met him in 2012, for example, he had just returned from a Medtronic-sponsored skills-based volunteering trip to Dr. Mohan's Diabetes Specialties Centre in Chennai, India. He told me about an amazing movement of DIY engineers he had discovered, who were individually and collectively trying to hack their own solutions to problems that weren't being addressed by large corporations. Noticing that many of them had similar hopes—for diabetes management apps for their smartphones—Desborough found the inspiration for his next project.

THE SHIFT: ENGAGE PASSION AND PURPOSE

From	To
Expertise above all	Purpose and passion at the center
CEOs wary of change	CEOs enabling internal disruption
Extrinsic motivation	Intrinsic motivation
Desire to create a successful product	Desire to solve problems

Passion Fuels Progress

Passion is what motivates intrapreneurs to keep going when the work seems thankless or when seemingly insurmountable challenges arise. Ravi Ramaswamy at Philips told me, for example, that when one of his teams unexpectedly lost a key member because of an internal transfer and everyone was frazzled by pressures in their usual jobs, "what kept us together was the passion" for delivering something that was "going to be radically different."

Passion is also, in many cases, the *source* of those radically different and valuable ideas. Lane Desborough is a prime example of an intrapreneur who spotted a solution thanks to a deep commitment to helping those who needed it. Balanda Atis, the chemist who formulated new foundation makeup for L'Oréal, is another innovator inspired by passion. Atis came to the company in the first place because, in her words, "I wanted to create cosmetics and combine my passion for science with my passion for makeup." Those two passions combined with yet a third when she saw the chance to create much better products for women of color.

Beyond motivating and inspiring intrapreneurs themselves, passion is a big part of why they are able to infect others around them with enthusiasm for their projects and keep them collaborating productively. Often, when ad hoc groups come together from different functional areas of an organization, members' incentives are not sufficiently aligned to guarantee that they will cohere. But if they are all personally committed to solving a certain problem for a certain community—if they share a common passion—mutual trust grows, and they can often find a way to overcome whatever frictions arise from their different roles and reporting structures.

Where does passion come from? Often, as so many of these examples show, personal experience plays a role. In the case of Ramaswamy, he felt a special motivation to work on a low-cost electrocardiogram device for rural Indian clinics. "I lost my dad because of a cardiac event," he told me. "If the ECG machine had been there—maybe, possibly, we could have saved him." But it is also easy to see how almost anyone could be inspired by the challenge of making medical technology more accessible to patients in developing nations. In many cases, the goal of the initiative is inspiring enough to create passion in employees who haven't actually suffered or been close to someone who has suffered from the lack of good solutions. Seema Patel noted about the sector she works in that the people in it are "development professionals first" and only secondarily attached to the specific organization that employs them. Having that professional identity elevates their sense of mission and assigns a higher priority to it than to any one organization's success.

Many companies whose work is not so urgent on the face of it can also have missions that are genuinely inspiring. Take LEGO, where people see their mission as selling more than injection-molded plastic model sets. The company's hope is to "inspire and develop the builders of tomorrow." Even a company whose workspace might look like it's straight out of *The Office* can emphasize how it relieves pain points in its customers' lives. You might recall Jeff Zias's comments in an earlier chapter about the fact that Intuit's flagship products support finances and taxes—something no one loves spending time with. And he admits that these may appear "pretty boring" on the surface. However, the company's mission to power prosperity around the world is tied to critical things like money, time, and financial confidence—and that's something employees can really get behind. He has seen enough motivated workers at this point to know that passion can be fueled in different ways.

Zias doubts that many young people announce to their friends that they want to be lawyers when they grow up—and yet he sees many lawyers going about their work with passionate commitment. "It's because," he said, "there's passion that can be fostered around particular sets of skills." Working toward mastery in a profession, to be capable of ingenious problem-solving, can be hugely motivating. "What I've found at Intuit," he said, "is being able to get closer to a customer, or being able to exercise creativity around your own idea in a self-directed way, or developing new skills—those things are really big." So Intuit tries to provide an environment that fosters that by "giving people the time and freedom and structure to put that passion to work, in terms of being a better innovator for the company, and ultimately for our customers."

The point is that even in companies that don't seem to have wildly inspiring missions, intrapreneurs can have high levels of intrinsic motivation to pursue the core business of the enterprise. As head of Intuit's "unstructured time" program, Zias occasionally hears a question raised about just *how* unstructured the time should be. "Hey, Jeff, surely you don't mean I should go work on my *car* during my unstructured time," someone might phrase it, "because I'm passionate about *that*." But Zias said, almost to his surprise, that the question is never posed in seriousness, and people always seem to find a business problem to solve that creates genuine passion.

There is a corollary to this. Just as a company with more mundane products should not give up on having impassioned workers, an enterprise with an exalted mission should not assume that everyone has it at the forefront of their minds. It should find ways to keep emphasizing it. At USAID, for example, where no one should doubt that they are engaged in work that matters, Patel told me about the restorative effect it can have when a person is pulled away from their paperwork and reminded of their purpose. Whether it's the chance to participate in a design thinking workshop or go out and work with rural farmers for a day, the experiences leave even veteran staffers saying, "That was the best day I've had in the office in years. It reconnected me to purpose." Keeping that passion alive, Patel is convinced, is "a powerful driver for intrapreneurship. It's a powerful driver for creative ideas and a source of resilience as you bring ideas into fruition through a complex organization."

Social Intrapreneurship Drives Engagement

Michael Moscherosch is absolutely passionate about the work he is doing currently at Johnson & Johnson (J&J). With a background in chemistry, he's been with the New Jersey–based manufacturer of pharmaceuticals and consumer packaged goods more than twenty-three years, and he's spent many of them in product development for feminine hygiene products. Now he's leading J&J's collaboration with a nonprofit venture called Sustainable Health Enterprises to make affordable sanitary napkins for women in Rwanda out of plant fibers so cheap they have traditionally been thrown away.

Sustainable Health Enterprises—which goes by the acronym SHE—is interested in this work for a number of reasons, but top among them is the contribution it could make to women's economic empowerment. In Rwanda, fully 18 percent of girls and women surveyed by SHE had to forgo school or work because they could not afford to buy the pads that would allow them to move about freely.[2] That's bad for women and bad for Rwanda. For any solution to work, however, it has to be self-sustaining. In other words, it has to meet this social goal by generating revenues more than equal to its costs—it has to succeed as a for-profit enterprise rather than philanthropy. This makes SHE what is known as a "social enterprise" and its founders "social entrepreneurs."

By extension, it makes Michael Moscherosch and his teammates at J&J "social intrapreneurs." It's a term that has gained currency as companies, especially global ones, have become increasingly serious about sustainability and, more generally, corporate social responsibility with a twist, as they increasingly look at sustainable, market-based solutions like SHE. With those spaces opened up for employees to take initiative, intrapreneurs have dreamed up many ways for their companies to have more positive impact. One book on the trend offers this as a definition: "Social intrapreneurs lead change within their organizations, without formal authority, that aligns with core business objectives while also advancing a social or environmental outcome."[3] That describes the J&J team well. They are contributing their knowledge of manufacturing processes and equipment to improve quality and efficiency at SHE's factory in Ngoma, as well as their expertise in consumer research to refine the product and its packaging to meet environmental standards.

J&J has a formal social intrapreneurship program that annually recruits highly capable employees to work on initiatives like these, knowing that for most participants, these will be "passion projects." Moscherosch said that when the idea for the SHE collaboration came up, he was busy with other work but couldn't imagine *not* getting involved. "I love it so much," he had thought. "I'm just going to do it."

Sometimes these projects can be quite remote from the operating strategy of an enterprise, but they still make sense because the enterprise's infrastructure and assets can be leveraged to accomplish an important social goal. At Intuit in 2008, for example, an intrapreneur named Deepa Bachu wanted to help subsistence farmers in India, whose constant struggles to make ends meet seemed to have more to do with market failures than with any lack of skill on their own part. Far too often, Bachu and his team discovered, food was harvested only to be sold at loss-producing prices, or even to spoil, because the farmers had so little access to information about when and where purchasers were buying and how much they needed. As a reminder, Intuit's business is financial software—not farming or commodities exchange. Yet it had the skills to prototype a mobile app the farmers and their customers would find useful, then to program it, and finally to scale it up to an in-market solution. As Roger Martin of the Martin Prosperity Institute told the story, "Within a year of launch, Mobile Bazaar had 180,000 subscribing farmers, most of them acquired by word of mouth. They report that, on average, the service boosts their prices by 16 percent."[4]

These are hardly isolated examples. Social intrapreneurship has gained considerable traction, in part thanks to some high-profile organizations that promote it. At the Aspen Institute, most prominently, Nancy McGaw, a former Bank of America managing director, created the First Movers Fellowship Program, which awards fellowships annually to "exceptional business professionals (social intrapreneurs) who have demonstrated an ability and passion for imagining new products, services, and management practices that achieve profitable business growth and lasting, positive social impacts."[5] It's a great honor, but more importantly it gives these intrapreneurs space and support as they get to work on their next big projects. As of the summer of 2017, the program has brought 170 fellows through its one-year incubation process, representing 115 companies in twenty-one countries. Recently, the First Movers team took stock of what has become a very effective program and identified the success factors behind it. Among them is underscored its "deep connection to personal purpose." Much of what it delivers to participants is leadership development, but the reason it does it so powerfully is because the program "does not shy away from deep personal exploration, and the emphasis on reflection and values." By design, First Movers "helps Fellows connect with the passion and purpose that inspires their work."[6]

A theme that runs through social intrapreneurship is that it's not always the company's mission that an employee is most passionate about. Sometimes employees have their own passions and can see ways to mobilize the company's assets to serve them. A formal social intrapreneurship program like J&J's can channel that energy and keep great talent in-house; altruistic employees who want to have maximum impact may conclude it is better to stay inside their current organizations and leverage their scale, rather than leaving to start tiny efforts on their own. Social intrapreneurship programs can also be a means for companies to identify and develop employees with leadership potential, who will then be better equipped to lead intrapreneurial projects closer to the company's core. Especially in cultures where the antibodies against new initiatives tend to be strong, social intrapreneurship projects may perform this talent development role better than traditional intrapreneurship initiatives. Because these projects have the advantages of inspiring passion while stirring up less politics, and pursuing goals that aren't subjected to the usual business performance metrics, they are solid testing grounds for *Disrupt-It-Yourself* ideas.

The Problem with Passion: #WeAreNotWaiting

Could there possibly be a problem with passion? As valuable—and sometimes indispensable—as it is, passion can also present challenges to organizations. At the outset of this chapter, I shared Lane Desborough's story of working on a solution for his son's diabetes care. Better than anyone I know, Desborough illustrates how passion drives intrapreneurs to take on big problems and make significant progress. But you might have noticed that my account ended right after the mention of his next project. I never mentioned how the idea of enabling access to monitoring device data by people's smartphones paid off for Medtronic. That's because it didn't. Unfortunately, this turns out to be something of a cautionary tale in intrapreneurship because, when the idea was presented to management, it didn't generate enough interest. Desborough left.

Thoroughly frustrated with corporate processes, Desborough went out on his own and, after pulling together an able band of collaborators, created a solution called Nightscout. It is software available for free to anyone on the web, built with open-source code, which uploads data from continuous glucose-monitoring devices to the cloud, where authorized caregivers can view it in real time with an internet browser, phone, or other smart device. It was a simple product, with no warranties, no FDA approval to be used in making medical decisions, and a technical support function that consisted

BARRIERS TO ENGAGE PASSION AND PURPOSE

- Passion makes work more "personal."
- Passion projects need to align with core business and strategy.
- Apathetic or lack of a clear approach to passion sparks exits if an organization doesn't support ideas.

of a Facebook group. But for all those exhausted parents wishing for a reliable way to monitor blood sugar levels remotely, it was available immediately. Hence the tagline on the Nightscout website: #WeAreNotWaiting. In other words, customers, hackers, and family members are not waiting for large organizations to solve their problems and will tackle them on their own by building networks and leveraging technology. This impatience underlines the urgency for large organizations to ignite DIY innovation and support the passion of their intrapreneurs.

Meanwhile, Desborough in 2014 formed a technology startup called Bigfoot Biomedical in partnership with two other leaders in the space. His cofounders, Bryan Mazlish and Jeffrey Brewer, have very similar stories to Desborough's. Each has a child with type 1 diabetes, each spent years working within the existing establishment of diabetes care, and each had come up with an ingenious "hack" to improve diabetes management. (The name Bigfoot comes from the nickname Mazlish had in the industry when rumors circulated that someone had put together an effective automated insulin delivery system on a D-I-Y basis, but the inventor thought it best to keep a low profile.)

Desborough's is far from the only story of an impassioned employee who wound up leaving a big enterprise out of impatience or lack of alignment. Another one is John Wood, who used to be at Microsoft and left to start libraries in the developing world.[7] Another is Jim Ziolkowski, who quit GE's famed financial management program to found a nonprofit organization that creates after-school programs for urban teens.[8] The list goes on and on. It turns out that the top reason that enterprising employees leave, when they do, is because their passion makes them impatient for results they aren't granted enough license to go after.

Tomas Chamorro-Premuzic, a business professor and entrepreneur, reported that 70 percent of successful entrepreneurs incubated their business ideas while employed by someone else.[9] For whatever reasons, their employers were unable to keep them and their new revenue-producing idea. Gifford Pinchot III once interviewed more than a hundred entrepreneurs who had previously been employed full-time by another enterprise. He heard the same thing in every case: In those prior work settings they had brought ideas forward and had them shot down or ignored by people further up the ladder. Eventually they decided to stop beating their heads against the wall and go get things done on their own.

Passion, therefore, is a bit of a double-edged sword. As long as Desborough and others like him bring it to their work, they are highly motivated top performers. But the same passion can make them highly dissatisfied if they perceive that people around them don't recognize how important their project is to the company or the world.

Forward-looking companies are taking note; Medtronic and companies like them are increasingly recognizing the value of DIYers and intrapreneurially-driven ideas that are often rooted in deep need and empathy. Increasingly, they "have come to regard the DIY community as allies," rather than a nuisance, understanding that they can collaborate rather than compete—or at a minimum learn from each other. In some organizations, "company reps meet with DIYers regularly to help them better understand how new technologies . . . will affect their system." NightScout vice president Weston Nordgren told me, "All of the major [medical device] players are working with the #WeAreNotWaiting community on some level . . . and some have made it their mission to work with us."[10] These changes demonstrate two important shifts: (1) a clear understanding by large organizations that end-user needs must be experienced firsthand and not based on assumptions that are manufactured inside the four walls of the organization, and (2) a new and more open approach to hackers and DIYers who are a part of these communities.

Deb Sundal at UnitedHealth Group told me about two related problems she has observed with projects with passionate originators: "Oftentimes what you'll see is the people who are the most passionate, and who look at their project through the most personal lens . . . they're not willing to let it go." It isn't always the case that the person who hatched an idea has the capabilities to develop and lead it through its next stages. But if that person can't trust anyone else to carry the ball forward, the goal may never be reached. Also Sundal said she has seen the occasional project "either get killed, or die, because it *requires* that passionate person to be behind it." On a normal operating basis, the economics just don't work; it is only the team's willingness to go above and beyond that keeps the effort afloat. If a project's success can only be sustained by superhuman efforts, it simply isn't sustainable.

For one last perspective on the problem with passion, I'll turn to Scott Adams, creator of *Dilbert*. The cartoonist behind the popular office-based comic strip occasionally turns his hand to serious (more or less) management advice, and in his most recent book he included a brief chapter titled "Passion Is Bullshit." It's a more nuanced argument than it sounds, and the bottom line is this: "It's easy to be passionate about things that are working out, and that distorts our impression of the importance of passion." In his own various career adventures, Adams says, "Success caused passion more than passion caused success."[11]

I take his point, along with the implication that the main screen for whether a company should back an intrapreneurial idea shouldn't be the employee's level of passion going in. Along the lines of what Jeff Zias observed, it often serves employees better to help them focus on the opportunity to master satisfying skills than to urge them to follow their dreams. But I won't go so far as to agree with Adams that you should "forget about passion when you're planning your path to success."[12]

My research reveals that caring deeply about a project's purpose makes an intrapreneur more willing to take on degrees of risk that their colleagues would forgo. It is also a source of resilience when setbacks occur. Passion is one of those things that makes hard work worth doing. And although we can't force people to have passion, we can and should create support systems, structures, and guidelines that leverage the passion that exists and help it grow and spread as a core component of DIY innovation.

DIY Playbook—Engage Passion and Purpose

Recognizing the passion and purpose parts of intrapreneurship allows companies to think more broadly about how to match their people with the problems they care most about. For employees, having the opportunity to work on passion projects creates greater engagement. For companies, it makes the most of creativity and ingenuity. Here's how to put this win-win dynamic to work in a Disrupt-It-Yourself way:

1. Make Purpose Programmatic
2. Leverage Passion That Bubbles Up
3. Push Passion Viral

1. Make Purpose Programmatic

Create social intrapreneurship programs. One sure way to create passion is by emulating the social entrepreneurship experience inside your organization. After all, developing innovative programs to tackle social challenges can create just as much progress (and passion) when the idea and outreach begin within. As well as helping the enterprise do well by doing good, social intrapreneurship is a great proving ground for the organization's future innovators.

Support processes, resources, and networks. When passion for an idea begins to bubble up within the organization, support it by helping innovators recruit a team, gain traction with resources, and determine if and how the idea connects back to the business.

Share responsibility for making programs work. Intrapreneurs who participate in formal support programs at their organizations such as incubators or accelerator labs can be more than the recipients of time and training. They can become invested in making the program worthwhile and improving it for the future. Sometimes the mere mention of this shared responsibility creates a palpable shift in energy. Leverage this by making communication about the program a two-way street. Participants' evaluations of team calls, learning modules, labs, and more should visibly lead to course corrections in progress (so that the program obeys the "follow the learnings" model it urges participants to adopt).

2. Leverage the Passion That Bubbles Up

Recognize when passion reaches a fever pitch. When Lane Desborough walked away from an established organization to solve his son's urgent health problem on his own, he was not just following his heart; he was also innovating in an area that represented a bona fide business opportunity. Some 1.25 million Americans are living with type 1 diabetes.[13] Many of them have long yearned for the type of simple solution that Desborough eventually created. What might have happened if the medical device company where Desborough had worked had supported his passion? Would they have developed a breakthrough solution together faster? Organizations should take this cautionary tale seriously, along with the ideas of passionate innovators like Desborough.

Cultivate community among innovators. Use each person's passion to bring them together with other innovators. Rather than being content to serve isolated intrapreneurs with disparate visions and needs, find the common threads that allow communities to form. In doing so, create mechanisms that support collaboration and ongoing communication among passionate cohorts as they continue their work to solve problems and reach goals.

Engage in innovation therapy. Don't try to reduce intrapreneurship to a check-the-boxes exercise. Encourage people to feel real joy when they are making progress and allow them to share their misery when things aren't working. Strengthening relationships to support greater resilience often begins with displays of vulnerability in group workshops and labs.

Make intrapreneurship personal. I participated in a kickoff session at an incubation lab where the first interaction was an exercise where each participant created a visual "thought board" representing them. Each person took ten minutes to explain the significance of the images they chose. It broke down barriers and created a personal place of reference for each member of the cohort. Leaders, coaches, and others can create a sandbox with some guardrails that ensure relevance to the organization now or in the future, and whether they should keep learning or pivot. But beyond this, they should allow project sponsors to make big decisions—including when to pull the plug—to encourage autonomy and keep the intrapreneurs passionate about their work.

Keep people talking about their experiences. Intrapreneurial output grows with opportunities for interaction and reflection. A communication cadence can include weekly one-on-one check-ins with mentors to keep participants working mindfully. Having a real person to serve as sounding board and source of experienced counsel is invaluable to many intrapreneurs' experience.

3. Push Passion Viral

Emphasize storytelling. One of the best ways intrapreneurs can share their passion and enlist others in their cause is by creating a narrative. At Lowe's Innovation Labs, for instance, Kyle Nel put a lot of emphasis on storytelling, and he still does as CEO of Uncommon Partners. One of his goals was to enable people to have the "right conversations" about innovation ideas. The process he put in place has everything to do with storytelling. If a team in his lab wants to engage senior management in a discussion about using virtual reality on the sales floor, for example, they need to be able to tell a compelling story about how that solves a customer's problem—and by "story," Nel doesn't mean just a chronological series of events but "a real narrative—where there are characters, conflict, and a narrative arc."

In fact, Nel and his colleagues at Lowe's routinely began meetings with important stakeholders by having them read brief narratives of problems encountered and solved. He said their first reaction to being handed a booklet full of illustrated panels was to smile and say, "This is funny." But by the time they finished the story, "they were saying, 'Holy crap.'" In the case of one idea, he recalled the CEO of Lowe's getting to the end of the story, looking up, and announcing, "We're going to make this a reality before someone else does." Even Nel was amazed at how "it completely changed the conversation."

Teach the art of the pitch. Maggie De Pree, cofounder of a global learning community called the League of Intrapreneurs, wrote in *Fast Company*, "When you are a cubicle warrior—fighting to transform organizations from the inside, your ideas are only as good as your pitch. . . . Pitching isn't just a skill of entrepreneurs and those working to make change from the outside, but should be part of the DNA of anyone looking to create a shift within organizations." She told me that winning over top management decision makers requires a deft combination of the rational and the emotional—passion and purpose. The story intrapreneurs tell has to "connect with corporate priorities," but at the same time it must "be authentic." A compelling story not only paints a vision of a happy ending, but also "creates an underlying emotional connection" between the audience and the teller. And, therefore, De Pree urges intrapreneurs: "Don't be afraid to go personal."[14]

Use multiple formats to persuade. Back when Seema Patel's small team at USAID launched the Global Development Lab, they engaged a documentary filmmaker to create a pitch with real production value. It depicted problems in West African agricultural economics and in Bangladeshi disaster preparedness from the perspective of the people affected, and it showed how their lives improved when they had better access to information. Full-color and high-definition formats are an apt alternative for storytelling and one that conveys and elicits passion in a very powerful way.

Executive Scorecard

- As you build a Disrupt-It-Yourself engine, are you managing for passion as you manage projects?
- Are you responding with support when passion bubbles up and people come together around a problem?
- Are you tapping into engagement by allowing intrapreneurs to own the ideas and projects that fuel passion in them?
- Are you able to let people "get personal," share experiences, and solve the problems that mean the most to them?
- When employees bring their enthusiasm and ingenuity to the workplace, do you signal that they should check their emotions at the door, or do you find ways to build, channel, and share that passion?
- What systems and programs will you build to leverage passion?

TEN

Principle 8: Add Discipline to Disruption

About a dozen teams from Stanley Black & Decker's global offices are gathered in a conference center with top leaders and managers of the 175-year-old manufacturer of industrial tools, household hardware, and security products. A subset of the executives discusses emerging technologies like AI and blockchain. Another group takes the stage to describe the future business opportunities associated with surveillance and security. That team is followed by another, and the afternoon goes on like this—with enterprising intrapreneurs positing predictions and pitching ideas for innovations intended to keep their businesses competitive.

Stanley Black & Decker's CEO, Jim Loree, has emphasized organic growth through innovation on many levels since he took the top job in 2016.

This event and others like it are aimed at radical and disruptive ideas. The teams have just wrapped up a ten-week, innovation-focused process, or "Sprint," during which time they updated their knowledge of potentially transformative technologies, then worked intensively to anticipate how to leverage the opportunities. In other offices around the world, additional Stanley Black & Decker teams are working to propose ideas, engage in real innovation experiments, and learn as much as they can to solve customer problems.

In contrast to today's formal event, which is geared toward the exponential end of the innovation spectrum (that is, they partnered with ExO Works to focus on emerging technologies like AI and blockchain, with the intention of yielding a ten-times return), many of the other programs are dedicated to innovating the core business in a more immediate way, or experimenting with business model innovations that range from simple enhancements to radically new ways of doing business around the globe.

At the end of today's program, Loree comes up to the front to thank the participants. "It feels like Silicon Valley in here!" he declares. Then he makes an announcement that sends a buzz through the room. The leadership team will provide next-round funding for seven of the ideas that have been presented. Getting any one of these to market would be a difficult and audacious undertaking. But seven? Loree acknowledges that all of these might not be commercialized, but he stands firm that each merits deeper exploration and experimentation.

Under the banner of a recast mission statement—to provide the tools "for those who make the world"—Loree wants Stanley Black & Decker not only to deliver top-quartile financial performance and be socially responsible, but also to become known as one of the world's leading innovators.

This raises a question. What does it take to become a world-leading innovator, and what role can intrapreneurs play? It takes at least three things: multiple streams of innovation, an all-in organization, and enough discipline and flexibility to enable risk and measurement. What this amounts to is a careful balance between freedom and function to dial exactly the right amount of structure into a Disrupt-It-Yourself approach.

Manage Multiple Streams of Innovation

Should a company take its chances on bold new offerings aimed at enterprise-wide transformation, or is it enough to raise the bar on how it makes, moves, and sells the existing ones? Does an innovative organization put more emphasis on incremental endeavors that it can predict and control—or dramatic, disruptive innovation that may take on a life of its own?[1]

Stanley Black & Decker has embedded systems that enable all of these. In fact, there should be a full spectrum of innovation options for intrapreneurs in any organization, from eye-popping, potentially disruptive innovations to clever little hacks on existing solutions. They are all valid, and companies can create disciplined systems by thinking through three streams of innovation.

1. Core Innovation

This first stream of innovation consists of predictable, on-going attempts to innovate the core of businesses in a recognizable and incremental way. (Making a stapler that can't jam, selling potato chips in a resealable bag, etc.) Core innovation syncs with what the lean movement considers Horizon 1 innovation:

development plans and growth projections are known, risk is considered contained, and the activities are closely aligned with the core business.[2]

Take an electrostatic duster, for example. Sarah Windham, a senior public relations manager at Stanley Black & Decker, woke up one morning with an idea for exactly that. What does a PR person know about electrostatics or the engineering of appliances? Not a lot. But Windham was able to draw on existing expertise and equipment across several functions of the company and bring the idea far enough into concept development to create a working prototype. Windham's obsession (her word) with the electrostatic duster was part of a company-wide contest to encourage people to pursue innovative side hustles. Much to Windham's delight, her duster won the grand prize: keys to the company Tesla for a month.

Contests and other similar programs encourage core innovation from every employee and keep intrapreneurs stepping up with ongoing process and product enhancements.

2. Transitional Innovation

This second stream of innovation focuses on substantially extending existing businesses and core activities by adapting the traditional business model or significantly expanding the markets into which they reach. (Remember the team at Tide Spin that accessed a new segment of customers by providing outsourced laundry services?) Like Lean's Horizon 2, transitional innovation requires a larger leap than core innovation in terms of investment and risk, but it is still familiar because it connects to the core even as it broadens it by adjusting its approach to expand reach and revenue.

And my work with the company to "meet users where they

are" in rapidly growing emerging economies (chapter 7) also falls squarely into the transitional innovation category. In that instance, we started with what the business knows best—tools—and conducted fast and frugal experiments on location to extend the market and adapt the business model to end user needs. We contained costs by leaning heavily on existing resources such as tool expertise, technology, and brand, while remaining asset-light throughout. This approach kept our resource needs low as we leveraged learning to make every successive attempt more successful, ultimately resulting in entirely new business models.

Transitional innovation can be a growth engine. But even more, it creates a bridge between core and transformational innovation. It uses your existing knowledge and assets to expand your capabilities so that you are within reach of the new and nascent businesses of the future.

3. Transformative Innovation

The third stream of innovation introduces entirely new offerings. In some cases, it's intended to replace or disrupt a declining core business. This type of innovation looks a lot like a startup in terms of risk, resource requirements, and the leap of faith that is required. (Think Netflix, Airbnb, or Tata Motors' $2,000 Nano car.) Similar to lean's Horizon 3, transformative innovation can look nearly nothing like your core business. It needs to be carefully incubated and, most believe, kept separate in almost every way.

Stanley Black and Decker's ten-week innovation sprint focused on this particular stream of innovation. Yet, for most organizations, attempts at core disruption through transformative innovation are avoided, ignored, and sometimes buried—even when the organization or industry is in precipitous decline—because the effort is aimed at displacing the business they know best. In terms of balance, a smaller percentage of an innovation portfolio should focus on transformational innovation work. One respected precedent, based on research from McKinsey & Company, shows that "companies that allocated about 70 percent of their innovation activity to core initiatives, 20 percent to adjacent [transitional] ones, and 10 percent to transformational ones outperformed their peers, typically realizing an outperforming P/E premium of 10 percent to 20 percent.[3] This corroborates the assumption that all three are necessary but the balance matters.

When to Keep Innovation Separate

Managing three fluid streams of innovation as part of one disciplined program is possible as long as they are each structured to succeed. This points to the thorniest dilemma that comes up when companies innovate: Keep it separate from the core business, or keep it close?

The easy answer is this: core innovation stays inside the business, transitional innovation needs to connect to the core in some way, and transformative innovation should be managed and incentivized separately.

Core—keep it close.

Core innovations will most likely make up the bulk of your innovation portfolio, and they are never to be underplayed or underappreciated. Remember that Balanda Atis's foundation for women of color launched a whole new business line for L'Oréal. And a main reason it attained so much success? Because it was developed, launched, and promoted as part of a thriving cosmetics company. L'Oréal's existing expertise and built-up brand assets are part of what made a major innovation into a massive success. Building core innovations into the organization, then, enables shared resources and sets the innovation up to benefit from the existing business and vice versa.

While core innovations like this sometimes involve partnering with outside experts and tapping new pools of talent, for the most part they utilize knowledge buried in the organization's own ranks. They are spearheaded by motivated employees with great ideas based on their proximity to the real work of the company.

Transitional—keep it connected.

Transitional innovation is a lynchpin between the other two, and it is usually built out of the core business in some important ways. Take Tide Spin. They created a separate business entity and business model, but connected the business back to its P&G parent very clearly. First, they kept the Tide name—what bigger brand is there when it comes to laundry? Next, the team tapped their networks across the sprawling P&G organization for experience and advice on every aspect of their service operation. Finally, they shared the physical facilities with another P&G experiment. One could argue that Tide Spin looked more like a transformational innovation because of its structure and business model, yet its connection to the core meant it could leverage an enormous source of cost savings and thus be able to focus most of its thinking and resources on the customer experience.

Transformative—keep it separate.

Transformative innovations are so potentially disruptive to the core business that they need to be kept separate to be protected from the corporate antibodies that will be arrayed against them. In this case, the infrastructure that once provided economies of scale no longer matters now that communications and information technologies have brought down the transaction costs of working with outsiders and connecting to customers. As ExO Works founder and chairman Salim Ismail told me, what that installed infrastructure of big firms mainly does for transformative innovation is limit flexibility in organizations that are built for relative stability.

Ismail went on to say that transformative innovations intended to disrupt old models—especially ones derived from "exponential technologies" like AI, blockchain, etc.—almost always require skills and knowledge that no one has had the opportunity to gain fully inside the existing business. This, he says, is why you have to separate innovation into different streams—to take something to "10x its current performance." Initiatives too big to fly under the radar must have top management's explicit blessing, and potentially disruptive initiatives require physical separation from the "mother ship" to have a real chance of taking off. Ismail says that a transformative venture has to be set up "as far away as possible" from the rest of the organization, physically and operationally—and on top of that, when it grows into a mature, viable business, it must simply be spun out.

Each of these three streams must be managed differently due to their specific requirements for metrics, leadership, and risk tolerance. However, in some ways they're compatible and at times should be interwoven—with the right reinforcing mechanisms. Large companies still hold value that cuts across all three streams—whether it's their brand, distribution channels, sales force, or even preexisting knowledge. All of this serves as glue to hold the innovation program together even as some ventures are kept separate.

THE SHIFT: ADD DISCIPLINE TO DISRUPTION

From	To
Preserve the past—afraid of change	Take risks to build the future; willing to disrupt oneself
Limited range of innovation	Hybridity: simultaneously growing the core while building the future
Risk in trying something new	Risk in standing still

Create an All-In Organization: Culture and Structure

Every attempt at meaningful innovation should be part of a specific vision, where DIY empowerment defines the culture and creates a path for growth, learning, and engagement. Despite the barriers to success, companies that are serious about innovation must manage multiple streams at once. Beyond these being potentially compatible activities, I have seen times that each can be mutually reinforcing.

Aiming for transformational innovation and moonshots helps to create the next baseline for core or transitional innovation. It also sends an important and highly visible signal to people throughout the company that innovation is highly valued. The signal transmits farther than the walls of the organization too. When an innovation is audacious enough, it enhances the company's reputation in the eyes of the markets—both financial and talent. The bottom line is that all three streams are required to stay relevant, remain competitive, and create a core capability to Disrupt-It-Yourself.

In order to make this work, companies must attend to a few big-picture pieces of the puzzle that make disciplined innovation possible.

Structure

We have examined when and why to keep an innovation initiative separate, but it is just as important to structure innovation in a way that achieves value from the program as a whole.

Stanley Black & Decker's Jim Loree uses the word *hybridity* to represent managing innovation in a holistic, structured way that also fully benefits individual initiatives. A hybrid starts with disparate elements that together achieve a strength or identity that the individual components lack. For Loree, this translates to an innovation program capable of producing new concepts using a structured approach and then channeling them accordingly into the right stream.

It is important to note that I think of hybridity as a way to optimize all three streams of innovation. It is a way to manage them, not replace them. As part of this, Stanley Black & Decker has a dozen newly built Breakthrough Innovation centers dedicated to taking on more smart risk as well as thinking big about ideas along a broad spectrum from transitional to transformational innovations, including new products, services, and business models that can further strengthen its various businesses as well as meet new customer needs.

In an October 2017 earnings call, for example, Loree mentioned a breakthrough innovation called FLEXVOLT. Introduced in June 2016, this new battery technology can change voltages automatically when you switch tools. A game-changing development on its own, it was the first major output of a breakthrough innovation initiative Stanley Black & Decker launched in 2014. "It really was a major home run," he told analysts.

Although creating a better battery is arguably a transformational innovation, the organization ultimately embedded the resulting products into an existing business unit. FlexVolt's application (in power-tool battery packs) meant that marketers in their core business knew exactly how to launch it. Add that to their deep expertise in digital marketing (from its Atlanta Digital Accelerator innovation center), and it reads like a case study in leveraging existing assets to commercialize a transformational innovation. That's hybridity.

Loree said the same would be true for some other innovations they have in the queue—they would be created outside the core business but ultimately commercialized within the core organization. Meanwhile, other innovations in the works "are more on the periphery of our core," he explained, and you'll probably see "more of a Silicon Valley–like approach to commercializing" transformational innovation externally.[4]

This hybrid ethos depends on several elements that DIY innovators know well. First, flexibility: the structure builds in enough flexibility to allow each stream of innovation to leverage the strengths of the others. Second, transparency: although some innovation needs to happen

BARRIERS TO ADDING DISCIPLINE TO DISRUPTION

- Disrupting the core feels dangerous.
- Multiple streams of innovation are challenging to manage.
- Many companies lack clear strategy for innovation.
- Different skill sets are needed for transformative versus core innovation.

in stealth mode, knowledge and output don't remain buried. And third, air cover: Loree expects executives to support innovation and gives them the tools and permission to champion innovations from others.

Culture

Consider that one of the biggest turns in Sony's history, a triumph that brought it roaring back to relevance, was the advent of the Sony PlayStation—created by a then-junior staff member named Ken Kutaragi. Management didn't want to be connected with video gaming because it was considered a "toy," which would tarnish their brand perception of being a superior high-end electronics manufacturer. It's a fantastic success story, but to bring it to market, Kutaragi had to overcome resistance from every corner of the corporate culture.[5] So, how would one create the corporate culture in which Kutaragi's idea could progress more rapidly, even as an outlier relative to the organization's other offerings?

Each of the crucial culture maxims explored throughout this book fully apply—frugal, inclusive, permissionless, and so on, but managing multiple streams of innovation surfaces some specific additions.

The first is *equal value*. Creating an organization that is equipped to innovate holistically requires that each of the three streams should be similarly valued and equally regarded. Transformative innovation should be neither lionized nor demonized compared to other streams; ongoing core innovation should be neither elevated above the rest nor taken for granted. This tricky condition flows from the top down and should take into account several softer-side qualities, such as recognition and status, as well as solid requirements, like metrics and incentives. Assigning the same high value to each stream of innovation makes it far more likely that people will want to act in an intra-preneurial capacity and share their knowledge and ideas widely.

The next element is *equanimity*. Managing a robust inno-vation program requires organizations to remain steady amid uncertainty and open to some measure of risk. They need to be willing to look beyond established business practices and take bold measures to disrupt their everyday ways of working. In this case, it means leaders must provide inspiration and air cover, and have a clear vision that prioritizes innovation. This is eas-ier to achieve when equanimity is part of a clearly articulated and communicated strategy and baked into the organizational design. In other words, strategy and structure must act as rein-forcing mechanisms to guide innovative behavior.

Finally, creating a culture of innovation entails *openness*. Leaders need to suspend assumptions and judgment in the early stages of ideation and experimentation. They need to empower others to act and defer interference and delay ultimate decisions until there is enough data that innovators can learn something useful. This open (and open-minded) approach creates an inclu-sive culture that encourages ideation and collaboration, and it accelerates activity across all three streams of innovation because more people are empowered to innovate.

Structure and culture are two sides of the same company coin, and each should reinforce the other, just as each stream of innovation ideally can help the others be better.

Doubling Down on Discipline

Many of the intrapreneurs I know assemble their teams through a combination of informal relationships and pure serendipity. Like the old TV ad where chocolate accidentally collides with peanut butter, they stumble onto conversations and colleagues and come up with great combinations. That kind of kismet makes for great stories that serve to encourage the requisite blurred lines of organizational fluidity. But supporting fluidity should have more formality in it so it's more repeatable—more sustainable.

One way to formalize both fluidity and function is through the dedicated innovation units being established within so many companies. They "keep it fluid" and "add discipline to disruption" by systematically connecting intrapreneurs with the colleagues and resources they need, internally and externally. With a bird's-eye view of the core, transitional, and transformational innovation that is in play, these centers can provide training and mentorship, funnel information, translate lessons, and look for resources and expertise that can be shared.

This isn't to say that it is the only work that these hubs, garages, centers, and labs are designed to do. In virtually every industry, and in nonprofits and government agencies as well, managers are waking up to the fact that their companies have been optimized for efficiency—for stamping out yesterday's inventions ever more uniformly and at ever lower cost—and not as much for envisioning what customers need next. The outspoken management guru Gary Hamel once critiqued traditionally managed companies this way: "Every CEO will at least give lip service to the idea that the world is moving faster and that we need to do a better job at innovation. But if you go into the organization and ask people to describe their innovation systems and practices, you get blank looks."[6]

I heard the same message more recently from Larry Keeley, cofounder of Doblin, an innovation consultancy that is now part of Deloitte. He says companies mistakenly characterize their anemic innovation as a "culture problem." No, it is a structure problem, he said, referring to the mechanics of innovation, such as metrics, incentives, and rewards. Eric Ries, the management thinker most associated with Lean Startup methodology, often points out, in the context of established businesses, that innovation is the next function for top management to put in place, and internal entrepreneurship must be a core discipline. People think of the standard departments of companies—finance, marketing, human resources—as obvious headquarters functions, but it is important to note that they did not always exist. Someone had to recognize that these deserved to be designed and managed at a level that cut across individual business units. The same recognition, Ries argues, has to happen now that the biggest challenge facing managers is making innovation happen more reliably in large-scale companies that call for focused, disciplined innovation where companies that can achieve these simply innovate more reliably.[7]

The result is that companies are putting formal functions in place, and appointing high-level executives like chief innovation officers, to figure out what their goals should be and how they should be structured and shared. Here are a few samples of what this important new discipline looks like:

Innovation Labs

At Lowe's, Kyle Nel was hired as a lone-wolf idea guy to pursue some radical-for-retail notions, and he went on to build the company's Innovation Labs. He described to me the scope of what he was trying to do: "How do you create systems that allow you (a) to identify what to work on, (b) to help people—on all different levels, from the CEO and board down—understand and have a substantive conversation about the outcomes of what

183

you're trying to build (and not the steps along the path to build it, because that's unknown), and (c) to create new systems for getting KPIs and metrics of success, so you can see if you're on the right track. That's what I spent my time building, and putting a whole lot of process and rigor to."

While most of Nel's focus was on ideas hatched in the Innovation Labs and staffed from there with dedicated teams, Innovation Labs staff also play a role in encouraging people in other parts of the company to innovate. By hosting "inventors' sessions," they give people a taste of the principles and capabilities central to their approach, and help them advance ideas by applying the Labs' expert skills in prototype building, UX/UI design, and neuroscience tools. "We were trying to take these groups of people that normally wouldn't get together," he explained, "and focus them on a problem for a very specific period of time—and then let them get back to their regular job very quickly."

For many, it's a beginning that they will continue to pursue in intrapreneurial side projects. But Nel thinks the effect is broader than that. "People said quite frequently that those who interact with the Innovation Labs become more malleable. If they're doing stuff with the Labs, everyone becomes better, more flexible, more agile, in things not even related to the immediate projects they're working on."

Dashboards

Utilizing simple dashboards that can be easily customized creates instant discipline and data. Designed right, dashboards create a snapshot of clarity and visibility for senior leaders, help align stakeholders around results, and benefit intrapreneurs by making metrics easy to grasp and track. Salim Ismail, chairman and CEO of the ExO Foundation, describes it this way: "Just like how a car dashboard provides real-time information of your car's performance and health, a business dashboard provides fast feedback, which makes massive growth possible by revealing opportunities and threats in real time."[8]

Here's an example of a simple dashboard I use to track a variety of metrics and accumulate insight about innovation experiments. There are a myriad of metrics to track and ways to represent them, but the most important thing is that metrics give everyone a simple and clear way to understand where initiatives stand.

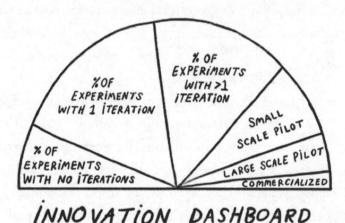

% OF EXPERIMENTS WITH >1 ITERATION

% OF EXPERIMENTS WITH 1 ITERATION

SMALL SCALE PILOT

% OF EXPERIMENTS WITH NO ITERATIONS

LARGE SCALE PILOT

COMMERCIALIZED

INNOVATION DASHBOARD

Sample the Startup Experience

Organizations such as TechStars serve as outside incubators that coach executives, help them nurture their ideas, and build up their skills. The former chief community officer of TechStars, Marc Nager, said one of the biggest benefits of this model is that it gets intrapreneurs and experienced founders together to share ideas and knowledge and generally get "revved up." It might be the first time an executive is exposed to the startup ecosystem, "and they tend to leave intensely inspired," not to mention educated.

"The idea is to take what really works in grassroots communities and organic ecosystems around the startup stuff and apply that lens to corporations," Nager told me. One particular program cofounded by Nager, called StartUp Weekends, offers an intense and immersive experience for executives.

"It solidifies the culture and gives them the vocabulary and some of the hard and soft skills, to key them up for a potential [intrapreneurial] journey," he said. After that, it's up to the individual to use that inspiration and knowledge to create momentum back at their organization. However, an important caveat is that the organization needs to have the right systems and structure in place, or any efforts at innovation will be wasted or kept undercover.

Startup Accelerators

Wayne Morris worked with the Startup Accelerator group inside SAP, which is situated within a complex, global organization that is broadly committed to enabling constructive disruption in a disciplined way. In fact, it has a clearly delineated set of steps that nevertheless allow for improvisation and high levels of creativity. For starters, the accelerator has a small "core team" that runs its process, but it supports "about a hundred others across the organization in different lines of business who have joined our community of intrapreneurs," Morris said.

Like many companies, SAP stages periodic "calls for ideas" to focus its seventy-seven thousand employees on new customer offerings and internal improvements. As part of that, Morris's group hosts ideation sessions to allow employees to sharpen their plan while coaches help them think about the recruiting they will need to do for talent and skills if their idea is selected for development.

The top teams are invited to participate in on-site sessions around the globe, and at that point the coaching becomes more intense, as each team must hone its idea and dig into the uncertainties that could affect their success. Those who get a thumbs-up are invited to participate in various camps, such as "acceleration camps," or enter into fellowships away from their jobs to work on a proof of concept. During that time, teams attend education sessions, participate in a "validation boot camp," and trade lessons learned with the other teams. Morris points to this peer support as a distinctive and important feature of SAP's model. The contacts made in these interactions enrich the networks these intrapreneurs draw on for their next projects.

Finalists go on to pitch in front of an investment committee—the business leaders who influence the destiny of the company.

"Having the opportunity to pitch your idea to these folks is amazing," he said, but the real value is in the learning and development. Reflecting on the Startup Accelerator process, Morris emphasized that it allows anyone to take their intrapreneurial potential to the next level. Not least because "it almost exactly mimics what happens in the real world to startups."

These are just a few of the distinct ways organizations create discipline to guide and encourage intrapreneurship at all levels. With some careful consideration, companies will arrive at whatever centers, systems, and scaffolds are right for them. And regardless of their form, they will have the best chance for success in organizations where the culture and structure support innovation. In addition, they will serve intrapreneurs best if certain principles guide their design—and one of the most important is being open and flexible enough for a Disrupt-It-Yourself approach. As part of that, I have seen that it is far riskier to refrain from innovating across the entire spectrum of horizons than to adopt a strategy that includes a diversified portfolio with the right dose of discipline.

DIY Playbook—Add Discipline to Disruption

The DIY approach requires structure and discipline in the right measure in order to extract the most value from each stream of innovation and install metrics that guide and measure success without losing the learning or limiting the idea. The prescriptive plays look like this:

1. Develop Multiple Streams of Innovation
2. Create a Culture That Enables Hybridity
3. Manage Disruption with Discipline

1. Develop Multiple Streams of Innovation

Turn intrapreneurship into the norm. Encourage the upstart ingenuity and disruptive ideas that will make you more competitive in the future. This includes creating the systems and providing the training and coaching to enable wide participation in intrapreneurial activities.

Shield transformational innovation from corporate antibodies. Moving aggressively into adjacent spaces and new ventures outside your typical purview attracts resistance. Initiatives that are too big to fly under the radar must have air cover from top management and be separated from the organization in order to have the best chance of taking off.

Think expansively about innovation. The three streams of innovation—core, transitional, and transformational—have different requirements and skill sets. But we need them all in order to succeed. A company can successfully reinvent itself and might still never learn how to effectively introduce incremental enhancements of its offering. Conversely, without periodically transforming itself in a dramatic way, companies may have no core to innovate. These are compatible streams of activity that are mutually reinforcing.

2. Create a Culture That Enables Hybridity

Send a strong message. Pulling off the occasional transformational innovation transmits an important and highly visible signal to people throughout the company that innovation is valued. The impact transcends the walls of the organization too. When an innovation is audacious enough, it enhances the company's reputation in the eyes of markets and employees.

Bridge insight gaps. Each stream of innovation requires different skills and resources. Yet they yield a common treasure—insight. One sure way to encourage innovation and enable success is to share best practices, success stories, and even cautionary tales across streams and throughout the organization.

Value innovation equally. The three streams of innovation are more likely to complement and reinforce one another when all are prized equally and incentivized appropriately. Eliminating favoritism for any one type creates a more supportive and active intrapreneurial ecosystem.

3. Manage Disruption with Discipline

Unleash innovation centers. Units dedicated to leveraging internal innovation can support intrapreneurship by identifying resources, offering training and mentorship, and creating a sanctioned path to develop and commercialize ideas. At the same time, beware of power plays and centralized control that can starve innovation instead of feeding it.

Know when to separate. When a transformational innovation has the potential to reinvent or even replace the existing business, organizations need to invest in skills, networks, knowledge, and resources. They also need to know when and how to spin off the venture for development and commercialization.

Customize KPIs. Create separate but appropriate metrics for each stream of innovation. In each case, knowing when to quit and leverage the learning is just as important as knowing what success looks like.

Executive Scorecard

- How do you tamp down the corporate antibodies that attack innovation within your walls?
- Does your organization appreciate core and transitional innovation and is it set up for its share of transformational innovations?
- How do the various streams of innovation complement each other, and what is your overarching plan to share learning and overlapping resources whenever possible?
- Do you partner with others outside the organization, instead of always going it alone on innovation, to quickly gain knowledge that isn't built into the organization?
- Have you experimented with innovation labs, incubators, or accelerators to send a signal across the company that innovation is both valued and expected?
- Do your best innovators mentor and coach the intrapreneurs who are just getting started?
- For more *Disrupt-It-Yourself* information including DIY workshops, keynotes, assessments, and e-courses, please visit www.blood-orange.com/DIY.

Eight Myths of Intrapreneurship

Look deeply into the subject of intrapreneurship and you find yourself confronted with contradictions. As I began work on *Disrupt-It-Yourself*, I pored over literature, read many accounts of classic intrapreneurial wins, and talked to people who have been involved in corporate innovation for years. I was inspired by the stories I heard of visionary employees who saw a need and managed to fill it, mainly through their own ingenuity and grit. Faced with resistance from colleagues, and with no expectation of resources or 20 percent time for exploration, they somehow beat the odds. They became the heroes of intrapreneurship.

At the same time, I started to doubt the mythology that has grown up around these heroes. Yes, many have been mavericks, iconoclasts, and dissenters. But in a twenty-first-century organization broadly committed to innovation—as many today are—would twenty-first-century intrapreneurs *have* to fly their pirate flag? And would that kind of person even have the same chances of success as someone on a more institutional path?

And what about all the people who have been properly supported in their efforts to discover new customer needs and deliver on them—maybe even working in formal innovation roles? Do they *not* deserve to be called intrapreneurs or DIYers because their work didn't involve pain and personal sacrifice?

It became clear that, in many ways, the intrapreneurial mythology we have inherited from the past is not serving us well today. It's more exclusive than inclusive—and it's making it harder for companies to innovate and grow.

With three years of research and reflection behind me, I'm convinced: It is time to construct a new mythology of intrapreneurship—one that celebrates the skills and behaviors that drive innovation forward today. We can start by taking a hard look at the old one. Here are eight myths about intrapreneurs that organizations must set aside in order to better support a Disrupt-It-Yourself environment.

Myth 1: Intrapreneurship is too creative for a disciplined approach.

At the core of an innovation is an act of creativity, and everyone knows that creative epiphanies are unpredictable. But that doesn't mean processes can't be outlined to take ideas to impact more reliably. Today, we know a lot more about how to do that. Design thinking, agile, and lean startup methods are all showing the results that can come when people are trained in an approach to doing things and get better and better at it.

> **Truth:** Innovation is too important
> to be done in a random way.

Myth 2: Intrapreneurs go it alone.

Today, when people hear the term *intrapreneur*, they think of the lone wolf—the voice in the wilderness proclaiming the value of an idea only he or she can recognize. In this scenario, the story of intrapreneurship becomes a hero's journey centered on a brave soul with the determination to single-handedly bring about change.

Based on cases I studied, that turns out to be a dangerous myth. Almost nothing of sufficient scale to move the needle on performance can be accomplished without teams of contributors, networks of partners, and committed sponsors providing air cover—and today's intrapreneurs are particularly savvy at navigating those networks. If we encourage people to go it alone, we keep them from developing the recruitment, leadership, and other skills that will allow them to grow as intrapreneurs.

> **Truth:** Intrapreneurship is a team sport.

Myth 3: Only "creatives" become intrapreneurs.

It's hard to call this a myth because creativity comes in many forms—but most people apply the term in a limited way. They often mean the kind of people who are overtly unorthodox in their thinking, appearance, and otherwise. But intrapreneurial success depends on the contributions of the "suits" as well as "creatives"—hipsters, hackers, and hustlers as well as those with more traditional business skills. And the right person to lead a team that combines various talents might not be the one with the most imaginative and original mind. It might be the one whose creativity helps them navigate the ins and outs of the organization.

Truth: Intrapreneurship requires a wide variety of talents and types. A successful intrapreneur can excel at any of them—and can't be expected to have all of them.

Myth 4: Management's best approach to intrapreneurs is benign neglect.

Most of the classic intrapreneurial projects we hear about and celebrate are ones that succeeded without management support. And the intrapreneurs who tell their stories usually say they were better off without it. But there's a problem with taking your lessons only from the initiatives that succeeded under such adverse conditions. We aren't hearing from all the ones that never made it. Intrapreneurship is best served by managers who both understand the value of it and know how to encourage it without taking charge of it. They help intrapreneurs actively and in many ways—from providing resources and connections to supporting their ongoing development and career paths.

Truth: Management's best approach to intrapreneurs is active support.

Myth 5: Intrapreneurs aren't in it for financial rewards, and they don't need performance metrics.

Intrapreneurship is a tough enough route that no one takes it without being intrinsically motivated. Passion is essential. But this doesn't have to be an either/or. Extrinsic rewards, whether an intrapreneur demands them or not, signal to the rest of the organization that this is important and valued activity. Performance metrics for innovation not only provide an objective basis for those rewards; they help intrapreneurial teams track progress toward goals and make the case for further investment—and DIY organizations understand this.

> **Truth:** If you want more of anything,
> measure it—and reward it.

Myth 6: Intrapreneurs are just like entrepreneurs.

Intrapreneurs are entrepreneurial in many respects, but that doesn't make the two synonymous. Both share a builder's mindset that makes them eager to create valuable solutions that don't yet exist. But intrapreneurs are less drawn to the huge rewards that can come with founding one's own firm. They don't want the all-consuming hours, unpredictability, and risk that go with that potential. Often they see a way to have more impact by staying in their jobs and leveraging their employers' already established scale and brands. They have the knowledge—and the patience—to navigate the politics and protocols of their large organizations.

> **Truth:** The typical intrapreneur is different
> from the typical entrepreneur in terms
> of both skills and motivation.

Myth 7: Innovation labs are the best place to house intrapreneurs.

This is a more contemporary myth, because it has grown along with the trend toward large companies, nonprofits, and government institutions creating innovation centers, labs, incubators, and garages. The whole point of these investments in facilities and talent is to focus on fueling the innovation pipeline. So this is where intrapreneurs should be housed, right? While that might seem true at first, the whole point of cultivating intrapreneurship is to encourage it across the organization. Creating a cordoned-off holding tank for intrapreneurs will signal the opposite and imply that innovation can only happen in specially designated spots by the people whose job it is to innovate. Innovation centers provide a clear pathway, training, networks, and other resources to help intrapreneurs succeed—regardless of where they come from.

> **Truth:** The place for intrapreneurs is everywhere.
> Innovation centers help provide the discipline
> and network required to grow intrapreneurial
> initiatives from idea to execution.

Myth 8: Having an innovation strategy has nothing to do with cultivating intrapreneurship.

Strategy is a top-down concept. It gets set at the highest level and cascades down into delegated tactics. Intrapreneurship, on the other hand, is bottom up. It's all about letting a thousand flowers be planted and seeing what comes up. These two concepts seem almost diametrically opposed, with very little chance of finding common ground. However, companies who want to see more intrapreneurial activity must have a clear strategy for achieving it—and what point could there be in disconnecting that strategy from the overall innovation strategy of the business?

> **Truth:** A clear innovation strategy is not only compatible with intrapreneurial activity—it is critical to taking intrapreneurship from a random event to a reliable engine of new solutions and revenue streams.

New mythologies don't emerge just because someone writes a book and suggests they are needed. The myths we carry around in our heads and choose to live by are harder to dislodge than that. They are formed over the course of years by a combination of our observations of what works and our values regarding how we wish things would work.

Right now, we are in a period when corporate innovation activity is exploding. We will have many more models of success, and of failure, to take our lessons from. Many new stories will emerge from which we can gain a new and better understanding—and with these we can construct a new mythology of intrapreneurship. Let's make it a good one.

Acknowledgments

It takes a village to raise a child. The same is true for a book—and for this book that couldn't be more true. Putting the *Disrupt-It-Yourself* ethos to work, I found tremendous community, collaboration, generosity, and deep pools of knowledge that scores of people were willing to share.

Profound thanks goes to my agent, Jacqueline Murphy, who went above and beyond—always—and was nothing short of a champion and intellectual partner throughout this entire journey. Very special thanks to my talented editor, Julia Kirby, who rode the at-times-rough waves of this process like a seasoned surfer, and always with aplomb. To Jim Loree, CEO of Stanley Black & Decker for his contribution of the foreword that so poignantly captures the essence of this book and is underpinned by intellect, awareness, and humility. To Jaime Ramirez, innovation leader and codesigner of so many of the lessons that went into this book.

Sincere gratitude to Brian Hampton, senior vice president and publisher at Thomas Nelson, for his interest and keen stewardship of the book starting at the acquisition stage. And to Jeff James, vice president and publisher at HarperCollins Leadership, for his expert guidance and unwavering support. Many thanks to my editor, Jenny Baumgartner, who thoughtfully asked all the right questions that made this book even better. To Sicily Axton and Hiram Centeno for tirelessly providing new ways of bringing *Disrupt-It-Yourself* to new audiences. To Brigitta Nortker and Karin Silver, my copy editors, for adding just the right changes to make the book sing.

To Julie Guggemos, for being a wise leader who graciously points the spotlight on others, allowing so many of us to catch some of her glow.

To Sam Reid, collaborator and friend, who has taught me that business is as much about understanding others—their needs, wants, emotions—as it is about the actual business itself. He has learned with me, and fielded even the most obscure questions with careful consideration, replying with incisive and relevant comments lined with wisdom.

To Hans Baelmakers of the Innov8ers Conference, who generously connected me to many interviewees during the research phase of this book, and to Kelly Schram, who helped to create a foundation for this book by introducing me to some of the first intrapreneurs I interviewed. And many thanks to my *Harvard Business Review* editor, Sarah Green Carmichael, for her help in shaping these ideas early in the process.

Thanks also to Malika Dale for sharing thoughts and ideas throughout, and to Steena Chandler for keeping this book on track with her organizational mastery.

To formal and informal collaborators Salim Ismail, Deb Sundal, and Stephanie Hammes-Betti, who shared the time, experience, and insights that line the pages of this book.

I must once again thank my family for their unwavering support and flexibility during what may have seemed like a never-ending process. My deepest gratitude goes to Hari, who fielded so many roles during the creation of this book: sounding board, idea engine, proofreader, steadfast supporter, and partner in celebrating even the smallest of victories.

Most sincere thanks to all of the disrupters and intrapreneurs who fought the hard fights and generously shared their knowledge, challenges, and questions with me to form the evergreen principles that shape this book—and to the leaders who are working to ensure that they eliminate barriers and support the human inside the employee as they build the discipline of innovation within their own organizations. Their work continues to inspire me.

Interview Index

The following individuals were interviewed across the period of March 10, 2015 to April 27, 2018. Organizations listed reflect each individual's role at the time of our interview.

Notes

Introduction

1. Julie Bort, "Retiring Cisco CEO Delivers Dire Prediction: 40% of Companies Will Be Dead in 10 Years," *Business Insider*, June 8, 2015, http://www.businessinsider.com/chambers-40-of -companies-are-dying-2015-6.

2. Scott D. Anthony et al., *2018 Corporate Longevity Forecast: Creative Destruction Is Accelerating* (Lexington, MA: Innosight, 2018), 2.

3. CB Insights, "State of Innovation Report: Survey of 677 Corporate Strategy Executives," accessed September 8, 2018, https://www.cbinsights.com/reports/CB-Insights_State -of-Innovation-2018.pdf?utm_campaign=state-innovation_2018 –04&utm_medium=email&_hsenc=p2ANqtz-97zzWnQE8gFc8 RagyLuupNEaj5mjKAjR39_enLlTJuIl82WIjFNQr5_Jg7plqPM gJC9I852lWqj6J8vF1M-JVVq7JQ9w&_hsmi=62319669&utm _content=62319669&utm_source=hs_automation&hsCtaTrackin g=c9680b05–8207–4149–8231-d7e711c3a30e%7C49e534b9 –8578–44a9-a8b8–5e9d703837ae.

4. Rob Shelton and David Percival, *Breakthrough Innovation and Growth* (PricewaterhouseCoopers, September 2013), https:// www.pwc.es/es/publicaciones/gestion-empresarial/assets /breakthrough-innovation-growth.pdf.

5. McKinsey & Company, "Innovation and Commercialization, 2010: McKinsey Global Survey Results," August 2010, https:// www.mckinsey.com/business-functions/strategy

-and-corporate-finance/our-insights/innovation-and
-commercialization-2010-mckinsey-global-survey-results.

Chapter 1: Navy SEALs, Not Pirates

1. Gifford Pinchot III and Elizabeth S. Pinchot, "Intra-Corporate Entrepreneurship" (unpublished white paper prepared for the Tarrytown School for Entrepreneurs, 1978). Gifford Pinchot went on to publish a best-selling book: *Intrapreneuring: Why You Don't Have to Leave the Corporation to Become an Entrepreneur* (New York: Harper & Row, 1985). Steve Jobs put the word into even broader parlance that year when he sat down for an interview with *Newsweek*, and *TIME* chimed in with John S. Demott's "Here Come the Intrapreneurs," February 4, 1985.

2. Pinchot, *Intrapreneuring*, 41.

3. For a more precise examination of the prevalence of intrapreneurs, see Niels Bosma et al., *Global Entrepreneurship Monitor: Special Report on Entrepreneurial Employee Activity 2011* (Global Entrepreneurship Research Association, 2013), available online 2015, https://www.researchgate.net/publication/258643022 _Global_Entrepreneurship_Monitor_Special_report_on _entrepreneurial_employee_activity. This 2011 study found that, even in the world's innovation-driven economies, no more than 4.6 percent of the adult population had taken a leadership role in some kind of entrepreneurial activity as employees in the past three years, and only 13 percent had participated in such initiatives (that is, not necessarily by leading them).

4. Rip Empson, "Instagram and Intuit Founders Discuss Lean Startups, Pivots, and What Makes a Product Successful," TechCrunch, September 13, 2011, https://techcrunch.com /2011/09/13/instagram-and-intuit-founders-discuss-lean -startups-pivots-and-what-makes-a-product-successful/.

5. Karl H. Vesper, *Entrepreneurship Education* (Wellesley, MA: Babson Center for Entrepreneurship Studies, 1985). More recently, Joe Abraham made the same point—that not all entrepreneurs are "wired" in the same way—in *Entrepreneurial DNA: The Breakthrough Discovery That Aligns Your Business to Your Unique Strengths* (New York: McGraw-Hill, 2011).

Chapter 2: Why Does It Have to Be So Hard?

1. Kim Sykes, "How Creative Problem Solving Unlocks Innovation," Batterii, October 15, 2015, http://blog.batterii.com/creative -problem-solvers.
2. Accenture Management Consulting, *Corporate Innovation Is Within Reach: Nurturing and Enabling an Entrepreneurial Culture* (2013), https://www.accenture.com/t20150523T 052044__w__/us-en/_acnmedia/Accenture/Conversion -Assets/DotCom/Documents/Global/PDF/Strategy_2 /Accenture-Survey-Enabling-Culture-Innovation -Entrepreneurialism.pdf.
3. As a recent example, Gallup's 2015 "State of the American Manager: Analytics and Advice for Leaders" reported on a survey of 7,272 US adults, revealing that fully half of them had left their job at some point in their career to get away from a manager they couldn't take. Access the report at Jim Harter and Amy Adkins, "Employees Want a Lot More from Their Managers," Gallup, April 8, 2015, http://www.gallup.com/businessjournal/182321 /employees-lot-managers.aspx.
4. Nitin Nohria and Ranjay Gulati, "Is Slack Good or Bad for Innovation?," *Academy of Management Journal* 39, no. 5 (October 1996): 1246, http://lib.cufe.edu.cn/upload_files/other/4_2014 0512035206_6.pdf.
5. Accenture, *Corporate Innovation*, 4.
6. James G. March, "Exploration and Exploitation in Organizational Learning," *Organization Science* 2, no. 1 (1991): 71–87.
7. Kavita Kumar, "Target CEO Unveils Next-Generation Store Concept," *Star-Tribune*, March 21, 2017, http://www.startribune. com/target-ceo-unveils-next-generation-store-concept /416665553/.
8. Nikolay Kolev, Andrew Goldstein, and Manuel Grossmann, "Five Insights into Intrapreneurship: A Guide to Accelerating Innovation Within Corporations," Deloitte Digital, 2015, https:// www2.deloitte.com/content/dam/Deloitte/de/Documents /technology/Intrapreneurship_Whitepaper_English.pdf.
9. Gordon MacKenzie, *Orbiting the Giant Hairball: A Corporate Fool's Guide to Surviving with Grace* (New York: Viking, 1998).

Chapter 3: Principle 1: Keep It Frugal

1. Navi Radjou, Jaideep Prabhu, and Simone Ahuja, *Jugaad Innovation: Think Frugal, Be Flexible, Generate Breakthrough Growth* (New York: Jossey-Bass, 2012).

2. Tom Kelley and David Kelley, *Creative Confidence: Unleashing the Creative Potential Within Us All* (New York: Crown Business, 2013), 126.

3. Greg McKeown, *Essentialism: The Disciplined Pursuit of Less* (New York: Crown Business, 2014), 5.

4. Martin Villeneuve, "How I Made an Impossible Film," TED Talk, February 2013, video, 10:55, https://www.ted.com/talks /martin_villeneuve_how_i_made_an_impossible_film.

5. See, for example, Martin Hoegl, Michael Gibbert, and David Mazursky, "Financial Constraints in Innovation Projects: When Is Less More?" *Research Policy* 37, no. 8 (September 2008): 1382–91.

6. See, for example, T. Baker and R. E. Nelson, "Creating Something from Nothing: Resource Construction Through Entrepreneurial Bricolage," *Administrative Science Quarterly* 50 (2005): 329–66. Meanwhile, any mention of bricolage should acknowledge the debt that management scholars have to anthropologists Claude Lévi-Strauss and Jacques Derrida, who developed the concept looking at other settings.

7. "Scramjets to Power Australian Space Odyssey This Month," UQ News, University of Queensland, October 22, 2001, https://www.uq.edu.au/news/article/2001/10/scramjets -power-australian-space-odyssey-month. The story is also shared in Peter Skarzynski and Rowan Gibson, *Innovation to the Core: A Blueprint for Transforming the Way Your Company Innovates* (Boston: HBR Press, 2008). Their takeaway from it is that "the correlation between innovation resources and competitive outcomes is much weaker than most people imagine" (p. 178).

8. Jessica Leber, "How Google's Moonshot X Division Helps Its Employees Embrace Failure," *Fast Company*, April 14, 2016, https://www.fastcompany.com/3058866/how-googles -moonshot-x-division-helps-its-employees-embrace-failure.

9. Sam Birchenough, reply to "How much would it cost if I want to hire a design company like IDEO or Frog Design to design a small electric appliance such as an electric toothbrush or a hair dryer?," Quora, April 30, 2016, https://www.quora.com /How-much-would-it-cost-if-I-want-to-hire-a-design-company -like-IDEO-or-Frog-Design-to-design-a-small-electric-appliance -such-as-an-electric-toothbrush-or-a-hair-dryer.

10. Ben Einstein, "Startups: Stop! Don't Hire a Design Firm!" *Medium*, December 23, 2013, https://medium.com /@BenEinstein/startups-stop-dont-hire-a-design-firm -7a7017a7a964.

11. Neil Tambe, "Bow Ties, Crazy Socks, and Hip-Hop: Tactics for Successful Intrapreneurship," *Neil Tambe* (blog), January 13, 2014, http://www.neiltambe.com/blog/2014/01/14/bow-ties -crazy-socks-and-hip-hop-tactics-for-successful-intrapreneurship.

12. "Meet David VanHimbergen of Tide Spin in Downtown," VoyageChicago, July 5, 2017, http://voyagechicago.com /interview/meet-david-vanhimbergen-tide-spin-downtown/.

13. Daniel H. Pink, *Drive: The Surprising Truth About What Motivates Us* (New York: Riverhead Books, 2009).

Chapter 4: Principle 2: Make It Permissionless

1. "About Grace Hopper," *CHIPS* (the US Department of the Navy's information technology magazine), June 27, 2011, updated March 2017, http://www.doncio.navy.mil/chips/ArticleDetails .aspx?ID=2265.

2. Mark Phelan, "Toyota's North American Staff Pitches in with Avalon Redesign for 2013," *Detroit Free Press*, June 24, 2012.

3. Alexis Ohanian, *Without Their Permission: How the 21st Century Will Be Made, Not Managed* (New York: Business Plus, 2013).

4. More details are available in the story posted by Jordan Cohen on the Management Innovation eXchange website: "Getting Rid of the Busy Work So You Can Get to Work," April 11, 2010, http:// www.managementexchange.com/story/getting-rid-busy-work-so -you-can-get-work.

5. Paddy Miller and Thomas Wedell-Wedellsborg, "Stealthstorming: How to Navigate the Politics of Innovation," *Forbes*, April 15,

2013, https://www.forbes.com/sites/iese/2013/04/15
/stealthstorming-how-to-navigate-the-politics-of-innovation
/#64ac1c7667fa.

6. Mitchell Weiss, "Lessons from Boston's Experiment with the
One Fund," *Harvard Business Review*, January 22, 2016, https://
hbr.org/2016/01/lessons-from-bostons-experiment-with-the
-one-fund.

7. Paul Rogers and Marcia W. Blenko, "Who Has the D?: How
Clear Decision Roles Enhance Organizational Performance,"
Harvard Business Review, January 2006, https://hbr.org/2006
/01/who-has-the-d-how-clear-decision-roles-enhance
-organizational-performance.

8. Bill Taylor, "How Domino's Pizza Reinvented Itself," *Harvard
Business Review*, November 28, 2016, https://hbr.org/2016/11
/how-dominos-pizza-reinvented-itself.

9. Rosabeth Moss Kanter, *The Change Masters: Innovation for
Productivity in the American Corporation* (New York: Simon
and Schuster, 1983).

10. Jon Ying, quoted in J. J. McCorvey, "Behind the Scenes at Dropbox
Black Ops," *Fast Company*, April 1, 2015, https://www.fastcompany
.com/3043856/behind-the-scenes-at-dropbox-black-ops.

11. Jeff Dyer and Hal Gregersen, "How Does Amazon Stay at Day
One?," *Forbes*, August 8, 2017, https://www.forbes.com
/sites/innovatorsdna/2017/08/08/how-does-amazon-stay
-at-day-one/#18ee29a7e4da.

12. Jay Greene, "10 Years Later, Amazon Celebrates Prime's
Triumph," *Seattle Times*, February 2, 2015, https://www
.seattletimes.com/business/amazon/10-years-later-amazon
-celebrates-primes-triumph/.

13. Dyer and Gregersen, "How Does Amazon Stay at Day One?"

14. Jonathan Bays, Tony Goland, and Joe Newsum, "Using Prizes to
Spur Innovation," *McKinsey Quarterly*, July 2009, https://www
.mckinsey.com/business-functions/strategy-and-corporate-finance
/our-insights/using-prizes-to-spur-innovation.

15. Anne Fisher, "How Adobe Kickstarts Innovation from its
Employees," *Fortune*, February 17, 2015, http://fortune.com
/2015/02/17/adobe-innovation/.

Chapter 5: Principle 3: Let Customers Lead

1. Design thinking is a discipline that has its origins in multiple places, but for an excellent introduction, see *Creative Confidence: Unleashing the Creative Potential Within Us All* (New York: Crown Business, 2013) by Tom Kelley and David Kelley. The latter is founder of both the design firm IDEO and Stanford University's Hasso Plattner Institute of Design, known as the d.school. The doctrine of the lean startup approach is from Eric Ries's *The Lean Startup: How Today's Entrepreneurs Use Continuous Innovation to Create Radically Successful Businesses* (New York: Crown Business, 2011).

2. Quoted in Jaime Sabartés, *Picasso: Portraits and Souvenirs* (Paris: L. Carré, 1946), chap. 7.

3. Mark Maletz and Nitin Nohria, "Managing in the White Space," *Harvard Business Review*, February 2001, https://hbr.org/2001/02/managing-in-the-whitespace. Emphasis mine.

4. Rip Emerson, "Instagram and Intuit Founders Discuss Lean Startups, Pivots, and What Makes a Product Successful," TechCrunch, October 2011, https://techcrunch.com/2011/09/13/instagram-and-intuit-founders-discuss-lean-startups-pivots-and-what-makes-a-product-successful/.

5. Vijay Anand, "Cheat Sheet to Create a Culture of Innovation," Intuit Labs (blog), *Medium*, May 2, 2014, https://medium.com/intuit-labs/cheat-sheet-to-create-a-culture-of-innovation-539d53455b53.

6. "Transforming Healthcare for Children and Their Families: Doug Dietz at TEDxSanJoseCA 2012," YouTube video, posted by TEDx Talks, May 19, 2012, https://www.youtube.com/watch?v=jajduxPD6H4.

7. Kapsin and her colleagues later published an analysis of the collaboration's results: Dana Etzel-Hardman et al., "Sedation Reduction in a Pediatric Radiology Department," *Journal for Healthcare Quality* 31, no. 4 (July/August 2009): 34–39.

8. Guy Boulton, "By Turning Medical Scans into Adventures, GE Eases Children's Fears," *Milwaukee Journal Sentinel*, January 21, 2016, http://archive.jsonline.com/business/

by-turning-medical-scans-into-adventures-ge-eases-childrens
-fears-b99647870z1–366161191.html/.

9. Alexander Osterwalder, "Corporate Innovators Need Access to
Customers," blog at Strategyzer, October 2, 2017, http://blog
.strategyzer.com/posts/2017/10/2/corporate-innovators-need
-access-to-customers.

10. The mind-set Davis is advocating has evidently been embraced
by Coca-Cola management all the way to the top. See
Keith Nunes, "Coca-Cola Co. Reimagining Its Approach to
Innovation," *Food Business News*, November 27, 2017, https://
www.foodbusinessnews.net/articles/10927-coca-cola-co
-reimagining-its-approach-to-innovation.

11. Olli-Pekka Kauppila, Risto Rajala, and Annukka Jyrämä,
"Antecedents of Salespeople's Reluctance to Sell Radically New
Products," *Industrial Marketing Management* 39 (February 2010):
308–16.

12. Heidi Gardner, Timothy Morris, and Narasimhan Anand,
"Developing New Practices: Recipes for Success," chap. 4 in
Managing the Modern Law Firm: New Challenges, New Perspectives,
ed. Laura Empson (Oxford: Oxford University Press, 2010).

13. Nicolas Bry, "BIG, Platforms of Opportunities for Breakthrough
Innovation at Pernod Ricard, with Alain Dufossé," *Rapid
Innovation in Digital Time*, October 23, 2014, https://nbry
.wordpress.com/2014/10/23/big-platforms-of-opportunities
-for-breakthrough-innovation/.

14. Quoted in Christine Crandell, "Customer Co-Creation Is the
Secret Sauce to Success," *Forbes*, June 10, 2016, https://www
.forbes.com/sites/christinecrandell/2016/06/10/customer
_cocreation_secret_sauce/#36c8b65b5b6d.

15. "DHL Innovation Day 2016—Challenge the Future," press
release, DHL, 2016, http://www.dhl.com/en/about_us/logistics
_insights/events/innovation_day/innovation_day_2016.html.

Chapter 6: Principle 4: Keep It Fluid

1. Brian Robertson, "History of Holacracy: The Discovery of
an Evolutionary Algorithm," *Holacracy* (blog), July 28, 2014,
https://blog.holacracy.org/history-of-holacracy-c7a8489f8eca.

2. "Holacracy and Self-Organization," ZapposInsights, accessed June 27, 2018, https://www.zapposinsights.com/about/holacracy.

3. Stanley A. McChrystal et al., *Team of Teams: New Rules of Engagement for a Complex World* (New York: Penguin Portfolio, 2015).

4. Deepak Mahadevan, "ING's Agile Transformation," *McKinsey Quarterly*, January 2017, https://www.mckinsey.com/industries /financial-services/our-insights/ings-agile-transformation.

5. Mahadevan.

6. Navi Radjou, Jaideep Prabhu, and Simone Ahuja, *Jugaad Innovation: Think Frugal, Be Flexible, Generate Breakthrough Growth* (New York: Jossey-Bass, 2012).

7. Normandy Madden, "Why It's Okay to Wash Potatoes in a Haier Washing Machine and Other Lessons from Philip Carmichael," *AdAge*, February 3, 2010, http://adage.com/china/article /china-news/why-its-okay-to-wash-potatoes-in-a-haier-washing -machine-and-other-lessons-from-philip-carmichael/141866/.

8. Andy Ellwood, "The Dream Team: Hipster, Hacker, and Hustler," *Forbes*, August 22, 2012, https://www.forbes.com/sites /andyellwood/2012/08/22/the-dream-team-hipster-hacker-and -hustler/#446e17be2c85.

9. Jeff Dyer and Hal Gregersen, "How Does Amazon Stay at Day One?," *Forbes*, August 8, 2017, https://www.forbes.com /sites/innovatorsdna/2017/08/08/how-does-amazon -stay-at-day-one/#18ee29a7e4da.

10. "The Manifesto for Agile Software Development" is available at http://agilemanifesto.org/. The website also provides information on its history and growing influence since 2001.

Chapter 7: Principle 5: Maximize Return on Intelligence

1. Janet H. Cho, "Reddit Co-Founder Alexis Ohanian Tells Case Western Entrepreneurs 'Don't Be Afraid to Fail,'" Cleveland. com, February 11, 2014, http://www.cleveland.com/business /index.ssf/2014/02/reddit_co-founder_alexis_ohani_1.html.

2. *Forbes* annually partners with the Innovator's DNA consultancy to produce its *World's Most Innovative Companies* list. See the methodology at "The World's Most Innovative Companies,"

Forbes, accessed July 2, 2018, https://www.forbes.com/innovative
-companies/#3f9924ed1d65.

3. Scott Kirsner, "What Big Companies Get Wrong About
   Innovation Metrics," *Harvard Business Review*, May 6, 2015,
   https://hbr.org/2015/05/what-big-companies-get-wrong
   -about-innovation-metrics.

4. Divina Paredes, "David Gram of Lego: An Insider's Guide to
   Radical Innovation," *CIO*, June 2017, https://www.cio.co.nz
   /article/620835/david-gram-lego-an-insider-guide-radical
   -innovation/.

5. For a good overview of how agile has moved beyond software and
   into innovation efforts of all kinds, see Darrell K. Rigby et al.,
   "Agile Innovation," *Insights*, Bain & Co., April 19, 2016, http://
   www.bain.com/publications/articles/agile-innovation.aspx.

6. Beth Altringer, "A New Model for Innovation in Big Companies,"
   Harvard Business Review, November 19, 2013, https://hbr.org
   /2013/11/a-new-model-for-innovation-in-big-companies.

7. "The Tata Group: Out of India," *Economist*, March 3, 2011,
   http://www.economist.com/node/18285497.

8. Jeffrey Rothfeder, *Driving Honda: Inside the World's Most
   Innovative Car Company* (New York: Penguin, 2015), 287.

9. Accenture, *Corporate Innovation Is Within Reach*, 3 (see chap. 2, n. 1).

10. Derek Thompson, "Google X and the Science of Radical
    Creativity," *Atlantic*, November 2017, https://www.theatlantic
    .com/magazine/archive/2017/11/x-google-moonshot-factory
    /540648/.

11. Tim Smedley, "'Intrapreneurs' Come to the Rescue," *Financial
    Times*, March 12, 2014, https://www.ft.com/content/556c3a46
    -8fdf-11e3-aee9-00144feab7de.

12. "'Culture Engineer' Astro Teller on Failure and Brilliance,"
    re:Work (Google), July 20, 2016, https://rework.withgoogle.com
    /blog/astro-teller-on-failure-and-brilliance/.

Chapter 8: Principle 6: Create the Commons

1. "Global Development Commons (GDC) In Brief," USAID,
   accessed September 11, 2018, http://pdf.usaid.gov/pdf_docs
   /Pnadk237.pdf, 1.

2. "3's Chief Design Officer Eric Quint Details the Firm's Creative Vision," *designboom*, https://www.designboom.com/design /3m-chief-design-officer-eric-quint-interview-11-10-2015/.

3. Poppy Lauretta McLeod, Sharon Alisa Lobel, and Taylor H. Cox Jr., "Ethnic Diversity and Creativity in Small Groups," *Small Group Research* 27, no. 2 (May 1996): 248–64, http://www. academia.edu/1325065/Ethnic_diversity_and_creativity_in _small_groups.

4. Roger C. Mayer, Richard S. Warr, and Jing Zhao, "Do Pro-Diversity Policies Improve Corporate Innovation?," *Financial Management* 47, no. 3 (Fall 2018): 617–50, http://onlinelibrary .wiley.com/doi/10.1111/fima.12205/abstract.

5. Megan Douglas, "Alumna Wins National L'Oreal Award," UA Little Rock, April 12, 2016, https://ualr.edu/news/2016/04/12 /alumna-wins-national-loreal-award/.

6. Both quotes come from a short film SAP made during the Intrapreneurial Program's 2016 "validate" stage of activity. SAP TV, "SAP Intrapreneurship—Validate 2016," October 20, 2016, video, 2:18, https://news.sap.com/sap-intrapreneurship-validate -2016/.

7. The story of Dave Myers's intrapreneurial effort on Elixir, and W. L. Gore's innovation culture more broadly, is well told in Alan Deutschman, "The Fabric of Creativity," *Fast Company*, December 1, 2004, https://www.fastcompany.com/51733 /fabric-creativity.

8. Nicola M. Pless and Thomas Maak, "Building an Inclusive Diversity Culture: Principles, Processes and Practice," *Journal of Business Ethics* 54 (2004): 129–47, https://pdfs.semanticscholar .org/6441/6f246c3583742372a6f44de7df0ceb5e8f93.pdf.

9. Nick Halter, "B-Dubs Fast Break Idea Came from the Bottom Up," *Minneapolis/St. Paul Business Journal*, July 14, 2016, https:// www.bizjournals.com/twincities/news/2016/07/14/buffalo-wild -wings-fast-break-idea-franchisees.html.

10. UQBATE Team, "Empowering Intrapreneurs," Deutsche Telekom, accessed June 28, 2018, https://www.telekom.com/en /company/thematic-specials/uqbate.

11. Gifford Pinchot reports that "the origin of the term

'intrapreneur' came from a white paper titled 'Intra-Corporate Entrepreneurship,' which was written by myself and my wife Libba for the Tarrytown School for Entrepreneurs in the Fall of 1978. That paper led to rigorous debate, the coining of the term *intrapreneur*, and eventually publishing of the book *Intrapreneuring* in 1985." The language here is from that original white paper.

12. Amy Edmondson of Harvard Business School is most responsible for laying the foundations of a theory of psychological safety. See especially Amy Edmondson, "Psychological Safety and Learning Behavior in Work Teams," *Administrative Science Quarterly* 44 (1999): 350–83.

13. Charles Duhigg, "What Google Learned from Its Quest to Build the Perfect Team," *New York Times Magazine*, February 25, 2016, https://www.nytimes.com/2016/02/28/magazine/what-google -learned-from-its-quest-to-build-the-perfect-team.html.

14. Janet I. Tu, "High-Octane Leader Drives Microsoft's Innovation Garage," *Seattle Times*, April 6, 2014, https://www.seattletimes .com/business/high-octane-leader-drives-microsoftrsquos -innovation-garage/.

15. For more on the role of "innovation catalyst" in particular, see Roger L. Martin, "The Innovation Catalysts," *Harvard Business Review*, June 2011, https://hbr.org/2011/06/the-innovation -catalysts.

Chapter 9: Principle 7: Engage Passion and Purpose

1. Scott K. Johnson, "Lane Desborough—Chemical Engineering and Diabetes?" Scott's Diabetes (blog), December 1, 2011, https://scottsdiabetes.com/2011/12/01/lane-desborough -chemical-engineering-diabetes/.

2. This came to the author from SHE founder, Connie Lewin, in an email on April 17, 2018. According to Lewin, the original research by SHE (Sustainable Health Enterprises) was conducted in 2008.

3. Gerald F. Davis and Christopher J. White, *Changing Your Company from the Inside Out: A Guide for Social Intrapreneurs* (Boston: HBR Press, 2015), 15–16.

4. Roger Martin, "The Innovation Catalysts," *Harvard Business Review*, June 2011, https://hbr.org/2011/06/the-innovation -catalysts.

5. "Nancy McGaw," Aspen Institute, accessed June 29, 2018, https://www.aspeninstitute.org/our-people/nancy-mcgaw/.

6. Shari Cohen, Eli Malinsky, and Jennifer Johnson, "Assessing the Impact: 2009–2016," Aspen Institute First Movers Fellowship Program, June 27, 2017, https://www.aspeninstitute.org /publications/assessing-impact-first-movers-2009-2016/.

7. John Wood, *Leaving Microsoft to Change the World: An Entrepreneur's Odyssey to Educate the World's Children* (New York: HarperBusiness, 2007).

8. Jim Ziolkowski and James S. Hirsch, *Walk in Their Shoes: Can One Person Change the World?* (New York: Simon & Schuster, 2013).

9. Tomas Chamorro-Premuzic, "How Bad Leadership Spurs Entrepreneurship," *Harvard Business Review*, September 10, 2012, https://hbr.org/2012/09/how-bad-leadership-spurs -entrepreneurship.

10. Naomi Kresge and Michelle Cortez, "The $250 Biohack That's Revolutionizing Life with Diabetes," Bloomberg Businessweek, August 8, 2018, https://www.bloomberg.com/news/features /2018-08-08/the-250-biohack-that-s-revolutionizing-life-with -diabetes?cmpid=BBD080818_BW&utm_medium=email&utm _source=newsletter&utm_term=180808&utm_campaign =businessweek.

11. Scott Adams, *How to Fail at Almost Everything and Still Win Big: Kind of the Story of My Life* (New York: Portfolio Penguin, 2013), 13–15.

12. Adams, 15.

13. The statistic was the latest as of this writing, published by JDRF, the leading global organization funding type 1 diabetes (T1D) research. "Type 1 Diabetes Facts," JDRF, accessed June 29, 2018, http://www.jdrf.org/about/what-is-t1d/facts/.

14. Maggie De Pree, "5 Ways Intrapreneurs Can Make the Business Case for Change at Their Company," *Fast Company*, October 29, 2013, https://www.fastcompany.com/3020777/5-ways

-intrapreneurs-can-make-the-business-case-for-change-at-their
-company.

Chapter 10: Principle 8: Add Discipline to Disruption

1. The terms *sustaining* versus *disruptive* are Clayton Christensen's favored language. In his theory of innovation, a sustaining innovation provides better performance to current high-end customers, whether the performance gain is incremental or a breakthrough improvement. Disruptive innovations do not bring better products and services to established customers in existing markets. They introduce novel solutions that displace current ones by being simpler, more convenient, and less expensive. See Clayton M. Christensen and Michael E. Raynor, *The Innovator's Solution: Creating and Sustaining Successful Growth* (Boston: Harvard Business School Press, 2013).

2. These three horizons are based on work by the consultancy McKinsey & Co. See Mehrdad Baghai, Stephen Coley, and David White, *The Alchemy of Growth: Practical Insights for Building the Enduring Enterprise* (New York: Basic Books, 2000).

3. Bansi Nagji and Geoff Tuff, "Managing Your Innovation Portfolio," *Harvard Business Review*, May 2012, https://hbr.org /2012/05/managing-your-innovation-portfolio.

4. "Stanley Black & Decker's (SWK) CEO Jim Loree on Q3 2017 Results—Earnings Call Transcript," Seeking Alpha, October 24, 2017, https://seekingalpha.com/article/4115837-stanley-black -and-deckers-swk-ceo-jim-loree-q3–2017-results-earnings-call -transcript.

5. For more details, see "PlayStation History Overview," Official PlayStation Museum, accessed September 11, 2018, http:// playstationmuseum.com/history/.

6. The quote comes courtesy of Curtis Carlson, former CEO of SRI International, who noted it from a talk Hamel gave and frequently uses it in his own presentations on applying best practices to innovation.

7. Eric Ries, *The Startup Way: How Modern Companies Use Entrepreneurial Management to Transform Culture and Drive Long-Term Growth* (New York: Crown, 2017).

8. Salim Ismail, "Dashboards: An Exponential Organization's Best Business Advisor," *Medium*, June 13, 2018, https://medium.com /@salimismail/dashboards-an-exponential-organizations-best -business-advisor-2be60d44cbda.

About the Author

Dr. Simone Bhan Ahuja is founder of Blood Orange, an innovation and strategy consultancy based in Minneapolis, Minnesota. She helps managers and leaders in Fortune 500 companies and other organizations develop big ideas and turn them into actionable plans. Past and current clients include 3M, Procter & Gamble, Target Corp, Stanley Black & Decker, Pepsi, and Medtronic—and many individual managers have also benefited from her keynotes, workshops, and assessments. She is a certified ExO instructor who helps top management teams consider how exponential technologies will disrupt (and allow them to disrupt) their businesses.

Ahuja coauthored the international bestseller *Jugaad Innovation*, called "the most comprehensive book yet on the subject" of frugal innovation by the *Economist*. She is a regular online contributor to *Harvard Business Review*, especially on the topic of how great organizations unleash the power of their purpose-driven "intrapreneurs" to drive innovation, deepen engagement, and achieve sustainable growth. Her work has also appeared in *BusinessWeek*, *Fast Company*, the *Economist*, and the *Stanford Social Innovation Review*.

About the Author

Ahuja serves as an advisor to MIT's Practical Impact Alliance and has also been advisor to the Centre for India & Global Business at Judge Business School, University of Cambridge. She is a member of the Board of Trustees at the Walker Art Center in Minneapolis. In all her work, she draws on her multidisciplinary education, including in traditional and improvisational theater, to bring a fresh yet practical approach to innovation.